George H. Horn

Revision of the Nitidulidae of the United States

George H. Horn

Revision of the Nitidulidae of the United States

ISBN/EAN: 9783741129858

Manufactured in Europe, USA, Canada, Australia, Japa

Cover: Foto ©Thomas Meinert / pixelio.de

Manufactured and distributed by brebook publishing software
(www.brebook.com)

George H. Horn

Revision of the Nitidulidae of the United States

B. caviColle n. sp.—Moderately elongate, rufescent, shining. Head sparsely punctate. Thorax one-fourth broader than long, sides parallel, slightly sinuate at middle, anterior and posterior angles rounded, margin posteriorly very obsoletely bidentate, disc flattened, at middle rather broadly concave and very sparsely punctate, at sides more densely and coarsely. Elytra scarcely wider than the thorax, each longitudinally broadly impressed near the suture, surface striate, striæ with moderately impressed but not closely placed punctures which become finer near the tip, sides with a few sparsely placed punctures. Body beneath nearly smooth. First ventral segment very sparsely and finely punctured, second, third and fourth each with a single row of closely placed deep punctures, last ventral sparsely punctate. Pygidium coarsely punctured. Length .09 inch ; 2.25 mm.

The concavity of the disc of the thorax, with its generally broader form readily distinguishes this species.

One specimen in my cabinet from Pennsylvania.

Revision of the NITIDULIDÆ of the United States.

BY GEORGE H. HORN, M. D.

Anterior and middle coxæ transverse, the former not prominent, posterior coxæ flat. Antennæ ten or eleven-jointed, capitate, straight. Tarsi usually five-jointed, nearly always dilated, first joint as long as the second ; rarely four-jointed *Cybocephalus* or three-jointed *Smicrips*.

The above short diagnosis sufficiently indicates the more important and defining characters of the family. For a fuller exposition the student is referred to the " Classification of the Coleoptera of North America."

With the exception of the two genera above indicated the family is quite homogeneous, including them as aberrant members there is no more heterogeneity than is usual in almost every family of large size. Mr. Murray (Monograph. p. 224), is willing to exclude *Cybocephalus*, basing his views on the four-jointed tarsi, the form of the thorax beneath and finally the general appearance, "to my eye *Cybocephalus* wants this family resemblance." The first objection is certainly entitled to a little consideration, but we are not informed where the genus is to be placed, if in a new family the precedent would require numerous new families everywhere among the Coleoptera from the Dytiscidæ down. The objection based on the structure of the thorax beneath is not at all valid, as *Cybocephalus* differs far less from *Amphicrossus* or *Cyllodes* than these do from *Nitidula*. Regarding the lack of family resemblance I am unable to see any feature which deserves more attention than another. *Pallodes* and *Conotelus* are certainly characteristic *Nitidulides* and do we not find *Cybocephalus* resembling *Pallodes* more than the latter does *Conotelus?* In the closely allied family Trogositidæ, we have *Trogosita* and *Thymalus* diverging far more in form than any two genera of Nitidulidæ.

In the exclusion of the Rhizophagini from the family I see no profit and no just grounds for so doing. The ten-jointed antennæ and the heteromerous male tarsi are for me entirely insufficient. That they form a step toward the Trogositidæ is true, yet the distance still remains sufficiently great.

As thus constituted the family may be divided into the following tribes :

Antennæ eleven-jointed, terminated by a three-jointed club.   Tarsi isomerous, similar in the two sexes.
   Tarsi five-jointed.
     Labrum free, more or less visible.
      Maxillæ with two lobes.   Antennæ feebly capitate...........**Brachypterini**.
      Maxillæ with one lobe.   Antennæ distinctly capitate.
       Prothorax not margined at base.   Head horizontal.
        Abdomen with two segments exposed..............................**Carpophilini**.
        Abdomen covered or pygidium partly exposed................**Nitidulini**.
       Prothorax margined at base, covering the base of elytra, head more or less deflexed..**Cychramini**.
     Labrum connate with the epistoma..**Ipini**.
   Tarsi four-jointed.   Body contractile.
     Thorax margined at base, covering the base of the elytra.....**Cybocephalini**.
   Tarsi three-jointed.   Body elongate...**Smicripini**.
Antennæ ten-jointed, club two-jointed.   Tarsi dissimilar in the sexes, heteromerous in the males...**Rhizophagini**.

The above arrangement is practically that of Erichson, with the addition of the two tribes.   Further comment on the tribes will be found under the head of each.

The Bibliography and Synonymy are deferred to the end of the essay, partly for convenience and also to free the student from the influence of names which may be attached to specimens, most of the collections of the country being in wretched confusion.

BRACHYPTERINI.

Antennæ eleven-jointed, terminated by a three-jointed (two in some *Cercus*) club, usually gradually formed and not of compact construction.   Labrum distinct, usually small, often deeply emarginate. Maxillæ with two lobes.   Anterior coxæ narrowly closed behind. Tarsi dilated.

The only character of any great value is that derived from the maxillæ, secondarily the form of the antennal club and the absence of grooves beneath the head.

In all the genera I find the males have a very distinct additional terminal dorsal segment, varying in size in each genus, being most distinct in *Anthonæus* and least so in *Amartus*.

Two of our genera are composed of small species, in which the elytra have a distinct marginal line and the epipleuræ consequently well marked, the other two have larger species, equalling in size any of our *Carpophilus*, in which there is scarcely any trace of marginal line and no very evident epipleuræ.

Brachypterus has the tarsal claws distinctly toothed at base, in the other genera they are absolutely simple or with merely a very slight dilatation.

The differences between the genera may be expressed in tabular form as follows:

Claws distinctly toothed at base.
  Elytra margined, epipleuræ distinct.......................................**Brachypterus.**
Claws simple or very nearly so.
  Elytra margined, epipleuræ distinct...**Cercus.**
  Elytra not or extremely feebly margined, epipleuræ indistinct.
    Form convex; terminal ♂ segment visible beneath only.........**Amartus.**
    Form depressed; terminal ♂ segment rather large, visible above.
                                         Anthonæus.

BRACHYPTERUS Kug.

Claws toothed near the base. Antennæ with a loose three-jointed club. Legs rather slender. Elytra much longer than the exposed portion of the abdomen. (Pl. III, fig. 2).

As recognized by Mr. Murray this genus is composed of very dissimilar material. The claws as figured, by no means represent the idea of a tooth as required by the generic description and the typical species, although the figure fairly resembles the claw of *Amartus tinctus*, in which the usual basal dilatation is present without any trace of tooth.

B. tinctus (Mann.) Murr., has been removed from the present genus and placed with another species in *Amartus* Lec., (= *Brachyleptus* Motsch., to which Murray assigned merely subgeneric value).

Three species occur in our fauna, all of small size and moderately robust facies, distinguished in the following manner:

Sides of thorax sinuate in front of posterior angles.
  Elytra truncate, sutural angle rectangular.................................**urticæ.**
Sides of thorax arcuate, hind angles obtusely rounded.
  Elytra truncate, sutural angle rectangular.................................**troglodytes.**
  Elytra separately rounded at tip, sutural angle slightly rounded.
                                      globularius.

B. urticæ Fab.—Oval, convex, piceous with slight æneous tinge, surface shining and very sparsely pubescent. Head coarsely and moderately densely punctured. Antennæ rufous. Thorax nearly twice as wide as long, convex, coarsely and moderately densely punctured, sides arcuate and slightly sinuate in front of hind angles. Elytra a little more coarsely but rather less densely punctured than the thorax. longer than wide conjointly, apices truncate. Abdomen above sparsely obsoletely punctured. Prosternum coarsely and densely punctured. metasternum sparsely punctured, abdomen more distinctly punctate. Legs rufous. Length .08 inch ; 2 mm.

The male has a very distinct terminal dorsal segment beyond the pygidium.

The sinuation of the thorax is by no means very evident but may be perceived by careful looking.

Occurs in the Atlantic States, probably introduced from Europe.

B. troglodytes Murr.—Very closely resembling *urticæ* but is a little more coarsely sculptured, and the sides of the thorax are not sinuate. The apices of the elytra are very squarely truncate. Length .08 inch ; 2 mm.

Widely distributed in maritime California.

B. globularius Murr.—Resembles the two preceding but is a little larger, the sculpture less evident and the pubescence faint. The sides of the thorax are not sinuate and the apices of the elytra less squarely truncate. Length .09 inch ; 2.25 mm.

Although very closely allied to the two preceding the species seems sufficiently distinct, rather from its general appearance than from the possibility of assigning any very definite characters to it.

Occurs in Colorado and Mexico, Mr. Murray says from Connecticut also, but I doubt the correctness of this statement.

CERCUS Latr.

The characters of this genus are given in detail in the books and do not require repetition. Certain matters however, appear to have escaped notice and deserve especial mention.

All authors who have had occasion to study Cercus, are in accord in being unwilling to assign the additional segment to the male. This is certainly incorrect in our species and probably also in all. The pygidium of the male is distinctly truncate and an additional segment is quite as apparent as in *Amartus*. In the female the pygidium is oval at tip and has a submarginal impressed line around the entire apical border. This line is interrupted at the middle or truncate portion of the pygidium of the male. Accompanying this sexual character is another in the form of the thorax. The males of two of our species have the hind angles of the thorax obtuse or even rounded, while in the females the sides of the thorax are

feebly sinuate and the hind angles distinct, almost rectangular. In
C. abdominalis this difference in the thorax is not evident. I am
not aware that any European species exhibits such sexual differences in the thorax, possibly they do not exist or such observers
as Erichson and Duval would have noticed them, while Mr. Murray
appears to have described the sexes of one of our species under
two names.

Cercus having simple claws is allied to *Amartus*, but differs from
that and *Anthonæus* in having but one abdominal segment exposed,
and the elytra being very distinctly margined at the sides, the
epipleuræ well defined.

The species occurring in our fauna are as follows :

Antennæ similar in the sexes.
  Club triarticulate; body above green or bluish glabrous.. ..**abdominalis.**
  Club biarticulate; body above not metallic, pubescent.
    Elytra sparsely punctate, that is the distance between the punctures is
      greater than the size of the punctures.............................**pennatus.**
    Elytra densely punctate, punctures closer together than their own dia-
      meter...**sericans.**
Antennæ dissimilar in the sexes, the first two joints dilated in the male.
    Elytra piceous with discoidal rufous spot on each...........**bipustulatus.**

C. abdominalis Erichs.—Oval, convex, metallic blue, shining, abdomen
and legs red. Head densely punctate. Antennæ rufous, club piceous. Thorax
convex, one-third wider than long, base a little wider than apex, sides moderately arcuate, feebly sinuate near the basal angles which are rectangular,
surface equally punctate, punctures moderately coarse not dense. Scutellum
sparsely punctate. Elytra a little longer than wide conjointly, sides feebly
arcuate, convex, a little more coarsely punctured than the thorax. Prosternum densely and coarsely punctured, body more finely and less densely,
abdomen moderately coarsely not densely punctured. Length .08—.10 inch;
2—2.5 mm.

The sexual peculiarities have already been remarked upon in the
generalities above.

Occurs everywhere in the United States east of the Rocky Mts.

C. pennatus Murr.—Oval, moderately robust, piceo-testaceous, moderately shining, sparsely pubescent. Head moderately densely punctate, front
feebly bi-impressed. Thorax nearly twice as wide as long, apex feebly emarginate, base slightly arcuate, sides moderately arcuate, margin narrowly
reflexed, posteriorly slightly sinuate ♀ or regularly arcuate ♂, disc convex, moderately densely punctate. Scutellum coarsely but sparsely punctate. Elytra longer than wide conjointly, apices rotundato-truncate, surface
moderately coarsely not densely punctate. Abdomen above very sparsely
punctulate. Body beneath sparsely punctate. Length .09 inch; 2.25 mm.
(Pl. III, fig. 6).

The males have an additional segment very plainly visible but less developed than in *Brachypterus*. To this species I have added *crinitus* Murr., it is the male.

Occurs from Canada to Tennessee and the New England States.

C. sericans Lec.—Oval, slightly oblong, usually testaceous, often with head and elytra piceous, surface feebly shining, sparsely pubescent. Thorax a little more than half as wide as long, moderately densely punctured, sides very narrowly margined, feebly arcuate, slightly sinuate posteriorly in the ♀. Elytra longer than wide conjointly, scarcely shining, surface densely punctured. Body beneath sparsely punctate. Length .06—.08 inch; 1.5—2 mm.

The sexual characters are in this species as in *pennatus*, in fact it was first observed that certain specimens here had a sinuate thorax while others were arcuate, and that while all the former were ♀ the latter were ♂ .

Occurs in California, rather widely distributed.

C. bipustulatus Payk.—Coarsely punctured, black; mouth, antennæ, legs and discoidal spot on each elytron rufous. Length .10—.12 inch; 2.5—3 mm.

The antennæ of the males have the first two joints much broader than in the female.

I introduce this species here on the authority of several specimens having been found near Boston. I do not know if it has obtained permanent lodgement.

AMARTUS Lec.

The characters of this genus are for the most part those of *Brachypterus*, the differences are as follows:

Two dorsal segments of abdomen exposed. Legs especially the tibiæ broader and stouter. Claws not toothed at base but with the usual dilatation. Third tarsal joint deeply bilobed. Elytra not margined, epipleuræ indistinct. (Pl. III, figs. 3—4).

The males have an additional abdominal segment belonging to the dorsal series, but in great part covered by the pygidium and visible only narrowly beneath. The pygidium does not differ notably in the two sexes and care must therefore be exercised in separating them.

It seems to me inexplicable why Mr. Murray allowed (*Strongylus?*) *tinctus* Mann., to remain in generic association with *Brachypterus*. The claws of the species being well figured by him and not exhibiting any basal tooth whatever in the sense in which it exists in *B. urticæ*, etc. Having admitted *tinctus* it is not easily understood why *Amartus* was not also joined. Synonymous with *Amartus* is *Brachyleptus* Mots., based on inaccurate characters given in a few words.

The facies of the species of the present genus is so remarkably different from *Brachypterus* as to indicate other more important differences, while the similarity between *rufipes* and *tinctus* is so marked that their close association cannot be otherwise than natural.

The two species above mentioned although very distinct on comparison are not easy to separate by tabulation, the principal differences are as follows :

Form very robust, thorax very convex, apex distinctly narrower than the base..**tinctus.**
Form less robust, more elongate, thorax moderately convex not narrower at apex..**rufipes.**

The second species has the habitus of *Carpophilus hemipterus*, while the former is much more robust than *C. melanopterus*. The two species belong to the fauna of maritime California.

A. tinctus Mann.—Oval, robust, piceous, subopaque, sparsely clothed with short greyish pubescence, surface densely punctured, the elytra a little more coarsely than the thorax. Thorax one-third wider than long, apex a little narrower than the base and very feebly emarginate, sides feebly arcuate, hind angles broadly rounded, base broadly arcuate and slightly sinuate each side, disc convex. Elytra as broad conjointly as long, slightly narrowed toward the apex, a feeble scutellar depression. Abdomen above very densely punctured, more finely than the elytra. Body beneath densely punctured. Length .16—.20 inch ; 4—5 mm.

The color is normally piceous above and beneath, but varieties occur either entirely ferruginous or with the legs and elytra of that color, (*ferrugatus* Murr.).

Occurs in California.

A. rufipes Lec.—Oblong oval, moderately convex, piceous, sparsely cinereopubescent, legs, antennæ, sides and apex of elytra ferruginous, surface densely punctured, opaque. Thorax one-half wider than long, apex scarcely narrower than the base, sides moderately arcuate, hind angles broadly rounded, base broadly arcuate, disc moderately convex. Elytra conjointly as wide as long, very little narrowed to apex, surface punctured as the thorax. Abdomen above densely and more finely punctured than the elytra. Body beneath densely punctured. Length .16 inch ; 4 mm.

All the specimens I have seen are similar in color.

Occurs in California, especially near Tejon.

ANTHONÆUS n. g.

Antennæ eleven-jointed, the last three joints feebly broader forming a loose club, the terminal joint conical and sub-appendiculate at tip. Mouth parts similar to *Brachypterus*, mandibles moderately prominent. First three abdominal segments short, the first longer than either of the two following, fourth equal to second and third together, fifth nearly as long as the first three. Tibiæ dilated, claws simple. Elytra not margined except very feebly near the humeri, epipleuræ indistinct. Thorax at base free.

The males have a sixth segment visible on the dorsal aspect of the abdomen.

The characters above given indicate a genus allied to *Amartus* by its mandibles prominent beyond the labrum, its simple claws and the presence of an additional segment in the male. It differs in the thorax being free at base, not overlapping the sides of the base of the elytra, its much more depressed form and nearly glabrous surface and the more prominent male segment. In *Amartus*, although the male has an additional segment, the pygidium is similar in the two sexes and in the male covers the additional sixth when viewed from above; beneath however the segment is visible. In the present genus the segment is quite as distinct as in *Carpophilus*, and the species might even be mistaken for a member of that genus. It has nothing in common with *Colastus* where Mr. Crotch placed it.

A. agavensis Crotch, (*Colastus*).—Oblong oval, depressed, piceous, varying to ferruginous with paler elytra, surface shining. very sparsely pubescent. Head moderately punctate. Thorax one-third wider than long, apex and base equal. sides regularly arcuate, angles obtuse, disc depressed, surface rather coarsely but not densely punctate. Scutellum punctate. Elytra a little longer than wide conjointly, slightly broader behind, surface moderately densely punctate. Abdomen punctured similarly to the elytra. Prosternum sparsely punctate, metasternum coarsely punctured at the sides, abdomen very sparsely punctate. Length .16—.18 inch; 4—4.5 mm. (Pl. III, fig. 5).

The additional segment of the male is oval, slightly concave, and not deflexed, the true pygidium is slightly emarginate.

Occurs in the flowers of *Agave* in southern California.

CARPOPHILINI.

Maxillæ with one lobe. Antennæ terminated by an abrupt three-jointed club, antennal grooves distinct. Tarsi dilated but sometimes feebly. Two or three segments of abdomen visible beyond the elytra.

These characters apply to the genera in our fauna, there being exceptional cases to one or other character among foreign genera.

It is worthy of special mention here that in all our genera the males have an additional segment belonging to the dorsal series beyond the pygidium. This additional segment seems to be constructed on the plan of a hollow cylinder closed at the distal end, and with a large fenestrum cut out of the lower side to allow of

the extrusion of the sexual organs and for the anal opening. This
cylindrical form is more or less modified in accordance with the
convexity of the abdomen; in a robust species like *Carp. pallipennis*
the cylindrical form is quite perfect, while in *Brachypeplus* and
Colastus it is very much flattened. A very good idea may be
obtained of the structure of this segment, by examining the terminal segment of the cylindrical larvæ of certain Elateridæ, such as
Agriotes or *Elater*.

The genera in our fauna are four in number and have represetatives
on both sides of the continent, excepting *Brachypeplus*. They are
distinguished as follows:

Ventral segments 2—3 short, first, fourth and fifth longer.........**CARPOPHILUS**.
Ventral segments 1—4 short, fifth as long as the others united........**COLASTUS**.
Ventral segments 1—2 short, 3—4 longer, fifth still longer.
  Body depressed; fifth ventral elongate but not conical......**BRACHYPEPLUS**.
  Body elongate, fifth ventral long and conical.........................**CONOTELUS**.

CARPOPHILUS Steph.

Labrum bilobed. Antennæ eleven-jointed, terminated by a flat-
tened-oval, three-jointed club, grooves moderately deep, convergent.
Legs moderately robust, tibiæ slightly broader at tip, spurs moderate.
Tarsi dilated, claws simple. Two sometimes three dorsal segments
visible beyond the elytra, abdomen beneath with segments 2—3
short, 1—4—5 longer.

This genus is closely related to *Colastus*, but differs in the structure
of the abdomen and the sexual characters. Here must be placed
Tribrachys Lec., the apparent equality in length between the first
three segments results from the extension of the abdomen in the
specimens on which it was founded.

The males have an additional segment beyond the pygidium, which
is strongly deflexed and apparently belonging to the ventral series,
an illusion which is further heightened by an emargination of the
fifth ventral in which the sexual segment closely fits. That it belongs
to the dorsal and not to the ventral series is easily proven by dissection, or by the position of the anal opening when the segments are
extended.

Several species have the middle tibiæ stouter in the male, this is
especially noticeable in *pallipennis*.

C. antiquus Er., is remarkable in having the posterior tibiæ suddenly dilated in its apical half, as in the male *Epuræa luteola* Er.
This was noticed by Murray who failed to recognize its sexual
nature.

The species of this genus are very troublesome to define, from their variability in color and their tendency to vary in sculpture. The following table will assist in their determination, and although prepared with considerable trouble is not a perfect guide but rather an aid.

Hind angles of thorax broadly rounded or very obtuse.
  Thorax evidently narrower than the elytra, disc subdepressed..........**yuccæ.**
  Thorax as wide as the elytra, disc convex.
    Thorax narrowed in front, anterior angles rounded.
      Elytra uniform in color but variable from piceous to yellow.
                      pallipennis.
      Elytra piceous with yellow basal and apical spaces.........**hemipterus.**
    Thorax quadrate, anterior angles distinct......................**mutilatus.**
Hind angles of thorax distinct but sometimes retracted.
  Sides of thorax with a short posterior sinuation, hind angles retracted.
    Robust, densely finely punctured, subopaque...............**melanopterus.**
    Oblong, depressed, sparsely punctate.
      Ferruginous, shining, elongate, prosternum smooth at middle.
                  tempestivus.
      Piceous, subopaque, oblong oval, prosternum densely coarsely punctured.
                  decipiens.
  Sides of thorax not sinuate, hind angles rectangular.
    Thorax very distinctly narrower at apex than base.
      Sides arcuate, surface opaque.. **niger.**
      Sides straight, surface feebly shining........................**marginatus.**
    Thorax subquadrate, not or very feebly narrower at apex.
      Surface opaque, densely punctured...........................**corticinus.**
      Surface moderately shining, sparsely or inconspicuously punctured.
        Prosternum in front nearly smooth.
          Piceous, nearly black, color uniform...................**brachypterus.**
          Piceous, elytra with large pale discal spot on each......**discoideus.**
        Prosternum in front densely, rather coarsely punctured.
          Punctuation of surface rather coarse and sparse. Hind tibiæ of male
            suddenly broader at apical half.................................**antiquus.**

C. yuccæ Crotch, (*Colastus*).—Piceous black, feebly shining, oblong oval, narrower in front. Head densely punctulate. Thorax one-half wider than long, slightly narrower in front, sides moderately arcuate, hind angles rounded, base slightly sinuate on each side, surface densely punctate. Scutellum moderately densely punctured. Elytra slightly wider than the thorax, a little longer than wide conjointly, apices obliquely truncate, surface densely punctured like the thorax. Abdomen above rather more sparsely punctured than the elytra. Body beneath densely punctured as above. Length .18—.24 inch; 4.5—6 mm.

The males present no special sexual characters other than the additional deflexed dorsal segment and the emarginate fifth ventral.

I cannot see why Mr. Crotch placed this species in *Colastus*, all the characters being those of *Carpophilus*.

Occurs abundantly in the Mojave Desert, in unopened flower heads of Yucca.

C. hemipterus Linn.—Piceous, oblong, feebly shining, sparsely pubescent, elytra with humeral spot and large irregular apical space testaceous. Head sparsely punctured. Thorax one-third wider than long, narrowed at apex, sides feebly arcuate, hind angles obtuse, base slightly sinuate each side, disc with a vague impression each side near the base, surface sparsely punctured at middle more densely near the sides. Scutellum sparsely punctate. Elytra conjointly wider than long, piceous, a humeral spot and large irregular apical space yellow, surface sparsely punctate. Abdomen above more finely punctured than the elytra. Prosternum coarsely but sparsely punctured. Body coarsely and more densely punctured. Abdomen sparsely and rather finely punctured. Legs pale. Length .16 inch; 4 mm.

In addition to the anal segment the males have the middle tibiæ stouter than in the female.

This species which is widely distributed over the region east of the Rocky Mountains, is very constant in its system of coloration, and by this may be known from any other in our fauna. It is nearly a cosmopolitan species.

C. pallipennis Say.—Form moderately robust, oblong oval, color variable, sparsely pubescent. Head coarsely not densely punctured. Thorax convex, one-third wider than long, narrowed in front, sides moderately arcuate, hind angles broadly arcuate, surface moderately densely punctured. Scutellum moderately densely punctured. Elytra conjointly a little wider than long, surface very regularly and moderately densely punctured. Abdomen above more finely and sparsely punctulate. Prosternum nearly smooth, body coarsely not densely punctured, abdomen more finely and sparsely punctured. Length .12—.16 inch; 3—4 mm.

The sexual characters are as in *hemipterus*, the middle tibiæ being even more dilated in the male.

The variations in color are so marked in this species as to have caused some synonymy. The most notable varieties will be mentioned.

pallipennis Say.—Piceous, abdomen beneath, legs and elytra yellow-testaceous. Immature specimens occur entirely yellow.

floralis Er.—Piceous, legs somewhat paler.

————.—Ferruginous brown, head and thorax somewhat darker.

Intermediate variations between these occur so that there is no lack of intermediate forms.

Occurs west of the Mississippi River from Kansas to Texas, thence westward through Arizona into the Peninsula of California, and southward through Mexico. It is abundant in the flowers of Cactus in the Spring.

C. dimidiatus Fab.—Oblong, color variable from piceous to ferruginous, very feebly shining, sparsely pubescent. Head moderately densely punctured. Thorax quadrate a little wider than long, sides nearly straight, hind angles obtuse not prominent, surface coarsely and moderately densely punctured, less densely punctured on the disc. Scutellum sparsely punctured. Elytra longer than wide conjointly, a little narrower toward apex, surface more sparsely and finely punctured than the thorax. Abdomen punctured similarly to the elytra. Prosternum coarsely and densely punctured, body less densely, abdomen moderately densely and more finely. Length .08—.14 inch ; 2—3.5 mm.

The males have the additional pygidial segment.

The nearly square thorax and comparatively large head distinguish this species from any other in our fauna. It varies considerably in color and size, so that the larger pale and the smaller dark specimens might easily be mistaken for distinct species.

Under this name I feel compelled to unite several species which Murray retains in a feeble manner as distinct. *C. luridus* Murr., is certainly not distinct from *mutilatus*, while *dimidiatus* is a smaller form of darker color often more sparsely punctured. A study of Murray's descriptions with the known tendency of that author to multiply species on a slender basis, leads me to believe that not only these but as many more species should be suppressed.

This species occurs everywhere in our country excepting the Pacific coast. Its original habitat was probably the West Indies, but it is now cosmopolitan.

C. melanopterus Er.—Oval, moderately robust, entirely pale ferruginous beneath and above, elytra usually piceous, the epipleuræ pale. Head moderately densely punctured. Thorax one-third wider than long, narrowed in front, sides feebly arcuate, hind angles small retracted, base slightly sinuate near the hind angles, disc convex, surface densely punctured, more finely than the head. Scutellum rather sparsely punctured. Elytra conjointly a little wider than long, slightly wider posteriorly, punctured similarly to the thorax. Abdomen above sparsely punctured and more finely than the elytra. Prosternum coarsely not densely punctured, body coarsely and more sparsely, abdomen rather finely. Length .16 inch ; 4 mm.

The middle tibiæ in the two sexes are similar.

C. rufus Murr., is a variety with the elytra ferruginous.

Occurs in Georgia, Texas and Mexico.

C. tempestivus Er.—Oblong, moderately elongate, pale rufous, suture and tip of elytra often narrowly piceous, shining, glabrous. Head sparsely punctate, antennæ pale, club piceous. Thorax broader than long, apex and base truncate, sides feebly arcuate, near base distinctly sinuate, hind angles retracted, small but acute, disc subdepressed, sparsely punctate. Elytra a little longer than wide conjointly, slightly narrowed at apex, surface a little more coarsely punctate than the thorax. Abdomen above a little more sparsely and finely punctured than the thorax. Prosternum smooth at middle, sparsely punctured at the sides, body and abdomen sparsely punctate. Length .08—.10 inch ; 2—2.5 mm.

There are no special sexual characters.

The three species associated in the table have very little in common except the sinuation of the thorax and the retracted angles, *melanopterus* being allied to *pallipennis*, *decipiens* to *discoideus*, while the present species stands rather alone, resembling feebly by its shining surface *antiquus*.

Occurs in the West Indies, Georgia and Florida.

C. decipiens n. sp.—Oblong oval, depressed, piceous, feebly shining, sparsely pubescent, elytra paler. Head moderately punctured. Thorax one-third wider than long, base slightly narrower than apex, sides moderately arcuate slightly sinuate posteriorly, hind angles distinct but slightly retracted, disc flat, surface not densely but equally punctate. Scutellum sparsely punctate. Elytra a little longer than wide conjointly, slightly narrowed toward the apex, surface more finely punctured than the thorax and distinctly alutaceous. Abdomen a little more coarsely punctured than the elytra. Prosternum, body and abdomen beneath moderately densely and equally punctured. Length .12—.14 inch; 3—3.5 mm.

Sexual characters as in *brachypterus*. The posterior tibiæ are also somewhat stouter in the male. This species resembles *discoideus*, but is distinct by the more evident punctuation of the surface, the sides of thorax perceptibly sinuate at base, the punctured prosternum, and the absence of discal elytral spot.

Occurs in California, at Tejon, in Arizona and Lower California.

C. niger Say.—Oval, slightly oblong, piceous, subopaque, sparsely pubescent. Head densely punctured. Thorax one-half wider than long, narrowed in front, sides regularly arcuate, base slightly narrowed and on each side sinuate, hind angles moderately prominent, disc slightly flattened, a feeble oblique impression at base each side of scutellum, surface densely punctured. Scutellum moderately densely punctured. Elytra conjointly as wide as long, slightly narrowed posteriorly, humeral angles prominent, disc slightly flattened, surface densely punctured. Abdomen above more finely and rather less densely punctured than the elytra. Surface beneath moderately densely punctate. Length .12—.18 inch; 3—4.5 mm.

The males have the additional abdominal segment; tibiæ similar in the sexes.

A specimen in my cabinet which I refer to this species as a variety has the elytra rufous in great part, the sides posteriorly, apex and suture being piceous, the legs also are rufous.

Occurs everywhere in our fauna from Canada to Arizona, and the variety above in California.

C. marginatus Erichs.—Oval, slightly oblong, sides of thorax and elytra continuous, rufous or rufo-piceous, tip of elytra somewhat darker, surface moderately shining, sparsely pubescent. Head moderately densely punctured. Thorax nearly twice as wide as long, narrowed in front, sides straight, slightly arcuate near the anterior angles, base nearly squarely truncate, hind angles rectangular, disc moderately densely punctured. Scutellum sparsely punctured. Elytra conjointly as wide as long, slightly narrowed posteriorly, sides feebly arcuate, apices squarely truncate, surface punctured as the elytra. Abdomen less coarsely and densely punctured than the elytra. Prosternum very sparsely punctured, body more coarsely and densely, abdomen less densely and more finely than the body. Length .06—.08 inch; 1.5—2 mm.

This is our smallest species and the only one with the margins of the thorax and elytra continuous, it has therefore somewhat the outline of an *Hydroporus*.

Middle and Southern States, not common.

C. corticinus Erichs.—Oval, slightly oblong, piceous, feebly shining, sparsely pubescent. Head densely punctured. Thorax one-half wider than long, as broad at apex as at base, sides feebly arcuate, hind angles rectangular, slightly prominent, base feebly sinuate each side, surface moderately densely, not coarsely punctured. Scutellum punctured at middle. Elytra a little longer than wide conjointly, sides feebly arcuate, slightly narrowed to apex, disc with a vague postscutellar depression, surface punctured like the thorax. Abdomen above more sparsely and finely punctate. Prosternum densely and rather coarsely punctured, body less densely punctured, abdomen less densely and coarsely. Legs rufo-piceous. Length .12 inch; 3 mm.

Sexual characters as in *niger*.

This species resembles a small *niger* but is known by the form of the thorax and the more shining surface, and excepting its shorter form resembles *Epurœa truncatella* in general appearance.

Occurs especially in the Middle and Southern States.

C. brachypterus Say.—Oblong oval, subdepressed, piceous, subopaque, very finely and sparsely pubescent. Head moderately punctate. Thorax nearly twice as wide as long, apex and base equal, sides moderately arcuate, punctures of the disc rather coarse and not dense, at the sides denser and finer, the interspaces alutaceous, hind angles small but distinct. Scutellum very sparsely punctate. Elytra a little longer than wide conjointly, slightly narrowed to apex, surface more finely punctured than the thorax, the intervals alutaceous, punctures rather coarser near the scutellum. Abdomen above a little more coarsely and sparsely punctured than the elytra. Prosternum nearly smooth, metasternum coarsely but sparsely punctured, abdomen less coarsely and more sparsely punctured. Length .10 inch; 2.5 mm.

The males are known only by the additional segment.

This species resembles *mutilatus* but is more elongate and has quite distinct thoracic hind angles. It is also difficult to distinguish from *discoideus* by description, but the latter is more depressed and broader, and the elytra have either a large pale clytral spot or are entirely pale.

Occurs from Pennsylvania to Canada and California.

C. discoideus Lec.—Oval, slightly oblong, depressed, color variable, elytra with discal paler spot more or less evident, surface moderately shining, very sparsely pubescent. Head sparsely, rather finely punctate. Thorax one-half wider than long, as wide at apex as at base, sides moderately arcuate, hind angles distinct, surface moderately coarsely and densely punctate, not more densely at the sides, intervals obsoletely alutaceous. Scutellum sparsely punctate. Elytra longer than wide conjointly, slightly broader behind, surface punctured similarly to the thorax but more obsoletely near the apex. Abdomen above more sparsely and finely punctured than the elytra. Prosternum nearly smooth, body sparsely punctate, abdomen more distinctly punctate, more densely on the last two segments. Legs piceo-testaceous. Length .10—.12 inch; 2.5—3 mm.

The males are as in *brachypterus*.

The color is variable from rufo-piceous to piceous, in the latter forms the elytra have a large discal pale spot on each, which is more or less distinct on all specimens.

The paler varieties of this species might readily be mistaken for *decipiens*, but the thoracic and prosternal characters will distinguish them.

Occurs from Tejon to Mariposa, California.

C. antiquus Mels.—Oblong, piceous, moderately shining, base of elytra rufous gradually passing to piceous. Head rather sparsely punctate. Thorax one-third wider than long, base and apex equal, sides feebly arcuate, hind angles rectangular, surface sparsely punctured at middle, more finely and densely at the sides. Scutellum sparsely punctate. Elytra longer than wide conjointly, slightly narrower toward apex, surface rather coarsely but sparsely punctate. Abdomen a little more densely punctured than the elytra. Prosternum and metasternum at sides coarsely and moderately densely punctured, abdomen less densely and more finely punctured. Legs rufous. Length .10 inch; 2.5 mm.

The males have the usual inflexed pygidial segment, and in addition the hind tibiæ are slender at base and suddenly broader at apical half as in *Epuræa luteola*. (Pl. III, fig. 21).

The color of this species is dark piceous, the anterior margin of the head and the sides of the thorax inclining to rufous. The basal half of the elytra is usually rufous, sometimes a narrow basal border only which extends along the sides and suture.

Occurs in the Middle and Southern States.

COLASTUS Erichs.

Our species are few in number and apart from the usual specific differences present no marked peculiarities. Their form is either broadly oval or oblong, usually much depressed, the surface punctured and sparsely pubescent. The prosternum at tip is very distinctly broader behind the coxæ, but in *truncatus* the anterior coxæ are very narrowly separated and the tip of the prosternum scarcely perceptibly dilated. In this species also the hind angles of the thorax are rounded, while in the others they are subacute and slightly prolonged backwards. The males are known by an emargination of the fifth ventral segment, which is at bottom either truncate or sinuate, and a small additional segment is visible which belongs to the dorsal series. (Pl. III, fig. 7).

The species known to us are distinguished in the following manner :

Hind angles of the thorax distinct.
  Scutellum smooth at tip.
    Form broadly oval.
      Thorax with an oblique fovea in each hind angle..................**morio.**
      Thorax without angular fovea; elytra maculate............**maculatus.**
    Form oblong, much depressed.
      Elytra rufous with entire limb narrowly piceous..............**semitectus.**
  Scutellum densely punctured.
    Form oblong; color uniformly piceous.........................**unicolor.**
Hind angles of thorax obtuse, rounded.
    Form oblong oval, depressed................................**truncatus.**

These species all belong to the fauna of the Atlantic region, but *truncatus* occurs also on the Pacific.

C. yuccæ and *agavensis* Crotch, do not belong to the genus, the former will be found in *Carpophilus*, the latter in the preceding tribe.

C. morio Erichs.—Broadly oval, depressed, piceous black, moderately shining, sparsely pubescent. Head coarsely and moderately densely punctured. Thorax more than twice as wide as long, sides arcuate, apex emarginate, base sinuate on each side, twice as wide as apex, surface feebly convex, coarsely and moderately densely punctured, a vague depression each side of the scutellum and a deeper oblique impression in each hind angle, the latter rectangular. Scutellum coarsely punctured, smooth at apex. Elytra conjointly wider than long, moderately densely and coarsely subscriately punctured, apices separately arcuate. Abdomen above less coarsely punctured than the elytra. Body beneath piceous. Prosternum very sparsely punctate, body and abdomen sparsely punctate, on the last segment more densely. Legs rufous. Length .16—.20 inch; 4—5 mm.

The males have the last ventral segment broadly but feebly emarginate, the emargination straight at bottom; a small additional segment is visible.

This species is at once known by its broad form and the oblique impression in the basal angles.

Widely distributed in the Atlantic region.

C. maculatus Erichs.—Broadly oval, depressed, sparsely pubescent, margin of thorax and four spots on each elytron rufous. Head and thorax as in *morio* but without the oblique angular impression. Scutellum sparsely punctured, smoother at apex. Elytra as in *morio* less densely and more irregularly punctured, surface piceous with four rufous spots, one in each angle. often confluent in broad vittæ. Abdomen above more sparsely punctate than the elytra. Prosternum nearly smooth. Body sparsely punctured. Last segment of abdomen with coarse rather sparsely placed punctures. Legs piceous. Length .16—.20 inch; 4—5 mm.

The male has the last ventral emarginate, a small additional segment visible, the emargination bisinuate at bottom.

Also of wide distribution, from the Middle States to Texas.

C. semitectus Say.—Elongate oval, much depressed, piceous, moderately shining, very sparsely pubescent, elytra reddish-yellow, sides and apex narrowly piceous. Head coarsely not densely punctate. Thorax one-half wider than long, sides moderately arcuate, apex narrower than the base, the latter feebly sinuate each side, surface rather coarsely not densely punctate, color piceous, lateral margins and hind angles usually paler. Scutellum punctate at base, apex smooth. Elytra conjointly very little wider than long, surface moderately densely punctate, the punctures subseriate near the suture, confused at sides and apex. Abdomen above more finely punctured than the elytra, and more sparsely placed. Prosternum very sparsely punctate. Body with coarse and moderately dense punctures. Abdomen less densely punctured. Legs piceous. Length .12—.18 inch; 3—4.5 mm.

The sexual characters are as in *maculatus*.

Of wide distribution in the Atlantic region.

C. unicolor Say.—Oblong oval, moderately depressed, piceous, subopaque, sparsely pubescent. Head moderately densely punctured. Thorax one-third wider at base than long, sides moderately arcuate, apex equal to the length base nearly squarely truncate, surface densely and moderately finely punctured. Scutellum densely punctured. Elytra conjointly a little wider than long, densely punctulate, a little more finely than the thorax. Abdomen more finely and sparsely punctured than the elytra. Prosternum very sparsely punctate. Body coarsely punctured. Abdomen sparsely punctulate, more densely on the last segment. Legs rufo-piceous. Length .16—.18 inch; 4—4.5 mm.

The sexual characters are as in *morio*.

This species is remarkably uniform in color, the upper surface being piceous black, the under surface somewhat paler.

Widely distributed in the Atlantic region.

C. truncatus Rand.—Oval, slightly oblong, depressed, pale rufo-piceous, sparsely pubescent. Head coarsely and moderately deeply punctured. Thorax nearly twice as wide as long, narrowed in front, apex equal to the length, sides moderately arcuate, base very feebly sinuate each side, hind angles rounded, disc feebly convex, surface moderately densely punctate. Scutellum moderately densely punctured. Elytra conjointly a little wider than long, apices conjointly emarginato-truncate, surface moderately densely and irregularly punctate. Abdomen more sparsely punctured than the elytra. Prosternum nearly smooth. Body coarsely and moderately densely punctate Abdomen sparsely, the last segment moderately densely punctate. Legs rufo testaceous. Length .08—.10 inch; 2—2.5 mm.

The sexual characters are the same as in *morio*.

This species is rufo-piceous or rufo-testaceous in color, somewhat paler beneath than above, often with the margin of the elytra darker than the disc forming the synonym *limbatus*, others have the elytra piceous with an oblique paler spot on each and form *obliquus*. I cannot find that these differ specifically from *truncatus*. It is worthy of mention that in this species the intercoxal process of the prosternum is very narrow even at its tip.

Very widely distributed, Canada to Florida and Texas, also in California.

A careful examination based on dissection shows that the males really do have an additional segment beyond the pygidium, which is deflexed so strongly as to become apparently a member of the ventral series. By softening a specimen and gently withdrawing this segment it is found to have a thorough membranous connection with the last dorsal, while the anus is very plainly visible between this small segment and the fifth ventral. From the depression of the body of most of our species, the deception concerning the relationship of this segment is even greater than in *Carpophilus*, but in *Brachypeplus* the same is again repeated.

BRACHYPEPLUS Erichs.

Labrum short, transverse, very feebly emarginate. Antennæ with suddenly formed three-jointed club, antennal grooves shallow, convergent beneath. Abdomen with three segments exposed beyond the elytra, beneath first two segments short, equal, third and fourth equal, each as long as the first two united, fifth equal to the third and fourth. Tarsi feebly dilated. Body much depressed.

The males have an additional segment beyond the pygidium which appears equally dorsal and ventral at the same time, but its true nature is that of an ultra-pygidial segment strongly deflexed as in *Carpophilus*, but even more so, with the anal opening between the posterior edge of the fifth ventral and the appendicular segment.

The affinities of this genus seem to me well marked. It and *Conotelus* are slight modifications of one type, and the differences are even feeble and may be narrowed down to an alteration in attenuation and depression and a slight variation in the form of the antennal grooves. Mr. Murray places the present genus in the *Late-fimbriata* and *Conotelus* in *Anguste-fimbriata*, yet an examination fails to show any reason for this, for we find that *Conotelus stenoides* is certainly as broadly margined as *Brachypeplus*. Following Murray, *Carpophilus* and *Colastus* are separated, but from the observation of material at my command these should be closely approximated at one end of a generic series, while *Cillæus*, *Brachypeplus* and *Conotelus* are in the other extreme. In fact Murray's "transition genera" show how little dependance can be placed on his two divisions above named.

We have but one species in our fauna.

B. glaber Lec.—Elongate, parallel, much depressed, reddish-brown, surface glabrous, abdomen piceous. Head moderately densely punctured. Antennæ rufous, club darker. Thorax quadrate, about a third wider than long, apex very feebly emarginate, base truncate, sides straight, very slightly arcuate in front, margin narrowly explanate posteriorly, hind angles rectangular, disc feebly convex, surface moderately coarsely but not densely punctured. Elytra a little longer than wide conjointly, surface striate, striæ indistinctly punctured, intervals flat with a series of moderately closely placed punctures. Abdomen above more finely.punctured than the thorax, beneath more coarsely punctured than above. Length .12 inch; 3 mm. (Pl. III, fig. 28).

This species belongs to Murray's division *Liopeplus*, and more closely allied to *rubidus* than any other. The other species of this group are known only from western Africa.

Collected by Hubbard and Schwarz, at Enterprise, Florida; extremely rare.

CONOTELUS Erichs.

Labrum short, transverse, feebly emarginate. Antennæ terminated by a three-jointed club of rounded or oval form, flattened; grooves slightly convergent passing backward toward the posterior border of the head. Abdomen elongated, three joints exposed above, beneath first two short and equal, third and fourth of equal length each as long as the first two together, fifth elongate, flattened conical, longer than the preceding two together. Tarsi dilated.

The males have the terminal dorsal segment truncate and feebly emarginate with a small additional segment exposed.

The species of *Conotelus* have an elongate form and resemble Staphylinidæ, recalling *Trogophlœus*. They divide themselves into two series according as the abdomen is margined or not, the character being really parallel with that existing in *Stenus*.

Our species are as follows :

Abdomen acutely margined. Head slightly prolonged behind the eyes.
Sides of thorax posteriorly sinuate. (Pl. III, fig. 11)................**stenoides.**
Abdomen not margined. Sides of thorax feebly arcuate. Eyes large occupying the entire side of the head. (Pl. III, fig. 10).
Legs testaceous..**obscurus.**
Legs piceous black.. ....**mexicanus.**

C. stenoides Murr.—Elongate, slender, piceous black, opaque, sparsely pubescent. Antennæ testaceous, club piceous. Head moderately densely scabro-punctate. Thorax a little wider than long, slightly narrowed toward the base, sides very feebly arcuate, at hind angles sinuate, margin moderately prominent and distinctly crenulate, disc depressed scabrous and vaguely punctate. Elytra a little longer than wide conjointly, finely striate, intervals with a row of moderately coarse elongate punctures each bearing a semierect hair, surface subgranularly alutaceous. Abdomen acutely margined, alutaceous and sparsely punctate. Prothorax beneath rugulose, body and abdomen sparsely punctate. Length .14—.16 inch; 3.5—4 mm.

This species differs from all the others in many important particulars, among which the smaller size of the eyes and the prolongation of the head behind them is worthy of notice, the sinuation of the thorax and its crenulated margin occur nowhere else, while the acutely margined abdomen occurs in several foreign species.

Occurs Texas and Central America.

C. obscurus Erichs.—Elongate, subdepressed, black, opaque, sparsely pubescent, legs testaceous. Antennæ testaceous, club piceous. Head finely scabrous, sparsely punctate. Thorax one-third wider than long, slightly narrowed in front, sides in front feebly arcuate, posteriorly nearly straight, margin narrow not crenulate, hind angles obtusely rounded, disc moderately convex, surface finely rugulose, sparsely punctate. Elytra nearly square, usually less black than the thorax, surface very finely granular with numerous irregular rows of obsolete punctures. Abdomen moderately shining, finely alutaceous, sparsely punctate. Prothorax beneath rather smooth, shining, body and abdomen sparsely punctulate. Length .14—.16 inch; 3.5—4 mm.

Occurs from the Middle States to Florida.

C. mexicanus Murr.—Black, subopaque, very sparsely pubescent. Head densely punctate. Thorax rugulose very obsoletely punctate. Elytra finely rugulose with a faint tendency to a linear arrangement. Abdomen above less shining than *obscurus* and more decidedly punctate, beneath also more punctate. Length .16 inch; 4 mm.

This species closely resembles *obscurus* in every way, but the head is more decidedly sculptured and the elytra less so. The legs are entirely black.

I refer our specimens to this species rather than give it another name as it corresponds very closely with Murray's description, and the species around it are so very closely allied that I prefer not to add a synonym to those which will result from a new study with more material than Murray had.

Occurs in south-eastern California extending southward into the Peninsula.

NITIDULINI.

Maxillæ with a single lobe. Elytra nearly entire allowing at most a portion of the pygidium to be exposed. Thorax at base not overlapping the elytra.

These are in short the only characters separating this tribe from the preceding. The genera composing it may be arranged in the following manner:

Prosternum depressed behind the coxæ, not prolonged..2.
Prosternum elevated behind, often prolonged...6.
2.—Tarsi very distinctly dilated on all the feet.. ......3.
   Tarsi not dilated or very feebly so..4.
3.—Antennal grooves strongly convergent.
   Labrum bilobed. Males with a sixth dorsal segment...........**Epuraea.**
   Labrum feebly emarginate. Males without sixth segment...**Nitidula.**
   Antennal grooves parallel, passing directly backwards............**Stelidota.**
4.—Mentum broad covering the base of the maxillæ..............**Prometopia.**
   Mentum not covering the maxillæ...5.
5.—Front not lobed over the antennæ.
   Mandibles with tip slightly bifid...**Phenolia.**
   Mandibles not bifid at tip...**Omosita.**
   Front lobed over the insertion of the antennæ.
   Mandibles simple at tip, toothed posteriorly.........................**Soronia.**
6.—Mesosternum not carinate.
   Head without antennal grooves.
      Anterior tibiæ not toothed externally...............................**Thalycra.**
      Anterior tibiæ bidentate at middle............................**Perthalycra.**
   Head with distinct antennal grooves.
      Tarsi not dilated. Body oval, pubescent.........................**Pocadius.**
      Front tarsi dilated. Body parallel and glabrous........**Orthopeplus.**
   Mesosternum carinate. Tarsi all dilated.............. ....**Meligethes.**

In those genera in which the tarsi are said to be dilated, the assertion applies to all the feet. In those with the tarsi not dilated it will be observed that the males do sometimes have dilated front tarsi.

On comparing this table with that given in the "Classification" p. 83. several changes will be observed. *Lobiopa* has been changed to *Soronia* the two genera not differing. *Thalycra* known also in Europe has been added, following it two new genera, *Orthopeplus* and *Perthalycra* are indicated. The latter genus was named but never described by the late Mr. G. R. Crotch, and I adopt in full his names as given in the "Check List," the species having become generally known under this designation.

Very little can be said of the genera in the way of comparison than is already made use of in the table. I was at one time led to believe that the degree of development of the sexual segment might

give some clue to a natural arrangement of the genera. This segment
is quite evident (nearly as much so as in *Carpophilus*) in *Epuraea* and
Thalycra, and either feebly evident or wanting in the other genera,
but in *Stelidota* one species has it quite well developed, the other two
not. The dilatation of the tarsi does not seem a very good character
inasmuch as the dilatation is apt to vary with the sexes and might
mislead, but as synoptic tables are intended as helps rather than certain keys, the student must acquire by practical application an amount
of experience which will enable him to avoid the errors necessarily
arising from the too literal interpretation of the tables.

EPURAEA Erichs.

Labrum bilobed. Mandibles acute at tip with a small tooth posteriorly. Antennæ with abrupt three-jointed club; antennal grooves
feeble convergent. Elytra truncate or entire. Tarsi dilated on all
the feet, sometimes feebly on the posterior.

Males with an additional anal segment, often with the middle and
posterior tibiæ dilated at tip.

Of all the genera this is probably the most troublesome in the
determination of the species, and their proper separation has cost
more time and labor than all the other genera together. All the
species described from our fauna have been seen by me with one
exception, this will be mentioned further on.

Mr. E. Reitter (Verhandl. des naturforsch. Vereius, vol. xii, Brünn,
1874), gives synoptic tables of the species of this genus dividing them
primarily into European and exotic, a procedure not warranted in
nature as several species are found around the globe in the northern
regions. During the next year (loc. cit. vol. xiii, 1875), Mr. Reitter
divides *Epuraea* into a number of genera on some characters which
our series shows to be extremely feeble and untenable, these are :

Omosiphora, based on those species with the posterior coxæ widely
separated, (*rufa*, *helvola*, etc.) This is a gradually evanescent character. Crotch in 1874, proposed the name *Epuraeanella* for these
species. *Haptoncura* is based on *luteola* and others with a supposed
larger labrum.

Micruria including *macrophthalma*, based on species with the claws
toothed. This is the species mentioned above as unknown to me and
it seems to me doubtful as a member of our fauna, one of the species
included in the genus being European, the others from Japan and
Madagascar. This genus is probably a valid one but the species is
probably not from our fauna.

In all attempts at an arrangement of the species of *Epuraea* which have been hitherto made, the extent of separation of the hind coxæ has been taken as a starting point, and this has been so magnified in importance that Reitter and Crotch have proposed to separate those species with distant coxæ under generic or subgeneric names. I am satisfied that any arrangement on this basis will produce anything but a natural sequence of species.

The sexual characters of the males seem to afford the means for a very natural grouping and as that sex have one peculiarity in common, the additional segment and special characters peculiar to series only, we have in the first instance the means of determining the males with unerring certainty and the group to which they should be referred almost as positively.

These groups may be defined as follows:

Middle tibiæ dissimilar in the two sexes, that of the male sinuate within an I thickened at tip, that of the female slender. (Pl. III, fig. 19).......Group I.
Middle tibiæ similar in the two sexes, slender.
Posterior tibiæ of both sexes similar and slender..............................Group II.
Posterior tibiæ of the male slightly arcuate, slender at basal half, suddenly broader at apical half. (Pl. III. fig. 20)......................................Group III.

These are the only groups known in our fauna, others occur in Europe with the femora dentate beneath or the posterior tibiæ toothed at middle, in the male.

GROUP I.

This group contains by far the larger number of the species in our fauna as well those of the greatest size. The middle tibiæ of the male are sinuate on the inner margin the apex being prolonged inward to a greater or less extent, the outer apical angle being obliquely truncate. This set of characters varies in the degree of development so that in *rufida* the middle tibia becomes deformed in aspect, while in *fulvescens* the sinuation is barely perceptible and the tibia seems to be merely stouter than that of the female.

The species arrange themselves in the following manner:

A.—Intercoxal process of abdomen broad, truncate.
Sides of thorax moderately arcuate, gradually broader to base.
Form oblong, color piceous, elytra conjointly not as wide as long.
monogama.
Form broadly oval, color yellow, elytra conjointly as wide as long.
Hornii.
Sides of thorax strongly arcuate, at base narrowed or sinuate, hind angles acute, slightly prominent.
Form broadly oval, elytra narrower at apex..........................**helvola.**
Form more oblong, elytra scarcely narrowed to tip........................**rufa.**

B. —Intercoxal process of abdomen narrow, acute, metasternum usually
    acutely notched posteriorly for its reception.

Elytra obliquely prolonged, not truncate.
    Middle tibiæ male feebly dilated at tip....................................**integra.**
    Middle tibiæ male rather strongly dilated..........................**ambigua.**
Elytra truncate at tip.
  Form oblong oval.
    Middle tibiæ ♂ strongly sinuate within, the inward prolongation of the
      tip well marked.
      Thorax broadest at base, hind angles rectangular.........**Erichsonii.**
      Thorax narrowed at base.
        The sides simply arcuate, hind angles not prominent.........**rufida.**
        The sides sinuate posteriorly, hind angles rather acute...**corticina.**
    Middle tibiæ ♂ feebly sinuate, the tip merely thickened.
      Thoracic margin explanate, usually sinuate near the base, hind angles
        subacute and prominent..**avara.**
        Club of antennæ dark...**immunda.**
        Club of antennæ pale...**adumbrata.**
      Thorax slightly arcuate near the base, the hind angles obtuse, margin
        not explanate...**fulvescens.**
  Form elongate, parallel. Middle tibiæ ♂ feebly sinuate.
    Joints 3—4—5 of antennæ moderately elongate.
      Surface subopaque, very indistinctly punctate. Thorax not sinuate
        posteriorly...**linearis.**
      Surface moderately shining, distinctly punctate. Thorax sinuate pos-
        teriorly...**truncatella.**
    Joint 3 only elongate, 4—8 short.
      Surface distinctly punctate. Sides of thorax slightly arcuate pos
        teriorly...**planulata.**

E. monograma Crotch.—Oblong oval, piceous, moderately shining, surface sparsely clothed with very short brownish pubescence. Head moderately
densely punctulate. Antennæ rufous, joints 3—4—5 equal, 6—7—8 equal, each
half the length of the three preceding joints. Thorax twice as wide as long,
sides moderately arcuate, gradually narrowed from base to apex, margin rather
widely depressed, slightly reflexed, apical margin moderately emarginate, base
sinuate on each side, anterior angles obtuse, posterior angles rectangular,
slightly obtuse, disc moderately densely punctulate. Elytra longer than wide
conjointly, slightly narrowed to apex which is truncate, margin reflexed, surface punctured similarly to the thorax. Body beneath moderately densely
punctulate. Intercoxal process of abdomen broad, truncate. Length .20 inch :
5 mm.

Male.—An additional small dorsal abdominal segment. Middle tibiæ sinuate
within, dilated at tip and prolonged inwards.

Female.—Abdomen without additional dorsal segment. Middle tibiæ simple,
gradually dilated from base to tip.

This is the largest species in our fauna, and may be readily
distinguished by its piceous color and the characters given in the
table.

Occurs in Vancouver and throughout the Sierra Nevada, in a

small white globular fungus growing on dead pines, each fungus
having a pair of the species.

E. Hornii Crotch.—Broadly oval, fulvous, feebly shining, surface sparsely
clothed with short fulvous pubescence. Head **sparsely punctulate**. Antennæ
fulvous, joints of funicle proportioned as in *monogama*. Thorax nearly twice
as wide as long, sides moderately arcuate and gradually narrowed from apex
to base, and with a feeble sinuation in front of the basal angles which are
small and acute, apex feebly emarginate, angles obtuse, margin flattened, more
widely explanate posteriorly and very slightly reflexed, surface moderately
densely punctulate. Elytra conjointly as wide as long, broadest near the
middle, apices rotundato-truncate, margin explanate and reflexed, surface
moderately densely punctulate. Prothorax beneath nearly smooth, at sides
transversely wrinkled. Abdomen rather more coarsely punctured than the
upper surface. Intercoxal process broad. Epipleuræ very sparsely punctulate.
Length .16—.18 inch; 4—4.5 mm.

The sexual characters in this species are the same as in *monogama*
and Mr. Crotch's remarks are erroneous.

The form of this species is nearly that of *helvola* but even broader
its color and size making it one of the most conspicuous species in
our fauna.

Occurs near Grimsby, Canada, whence specimens were sent me
some years ago by Mr. Johnson Pettit.

E. helvola Erichs.—Broadly oval, piceous brown, feebly shining, sparsely
clothed with short brownish pubescence. Head coarsely and densely punctured. Antennæ as in *monogama*, brownish, club darker. Thorax rather more
than twice as wide as long, apex deeply emarginate, base subtruncate, sides
strongly arcuate slightly narrowing at base, sinuate in front of the hind angles
which are subacute and slightly prominent, margin broadly explanate and
slightly reflexed, surface moderately densely punctate and subgranulate.
Elytra oval, a little longer than wide, narrower at apex, moderately convex
suture slightly elevated, margin reflexed but gradually evanescent to the tip
which is truncate, surface moderately densely punctulate with a **subgranular**
aspect. Body beneath moderately densely punctate. Femora rather **coarsely**
and densely punctate. Intercoxal process broad, truncate. Length .12 inch;
3 mm.

The sexual characters are as in *monogama*, but the sinuation
of the middle tibiæ and the prolongation inwards at tip still more
pronounced.

The color of this species varies somewhat, usually entirely piceous
brown, often with the entire margin and suture more or less rufous.
The hind angles of the thorax vary a little in the degree of their
prominence, as well as the sinuation in front of them.

Mr. E. Reitter (Verhandl. des Naturf. Vereines in Brünn, xii
has apparently separated two color varieties of this species, to one of

which he gives the name *helvola*, the other *rufa*, the true form of the latter being described as a new species.

Occurs abundantly in the entire region east of the Rocky Mts.

E. rufa Say.—Oval, rufo-piceous, moderately shining, sparsely pubescent. Head moderately densely punctate. Antennæ rufous, club darker, funicle as in *monogama*. Thorax rather more than twice as wide as long, very little narrower at apex than at base, sides strongly arcuate, obliquely narrowed and very feebly sinuate near the base, hind angles acute moderately prominent, margin moderately explanate but not reflexed, basal margin sinuate on each side, surface moderately densely punctate. Elytra oval, longer than wide, sides feebly arcuate and slightly narrower to base, margin narrow and slightly reflexed, surface irregular, densely punctate, apex rotundato-truncate. Body beneath moderately densely punctate, more coarsely than the upper surface. Intercoxal process of abdomen broad, truncate. Femora coarsely and densely punctate. Length .12—.14 inch; 3—3.5 mm.

The sexual characters are as in *helvola*, the inner edge of the middle tibia of the male being rather deeply sinuate and at apex prolonged inwards.

This species is often confounded with *helvola* in collections, from which however it abundantly differs in its more oblong form and longer elytra which are scarcely narrowed to tip and very narrowly margined. It has in some cabinets the *mss.* name *punctatus.* The determination of the synonym above has been made from a specimen received directly from Mr. Reitter, who places it erroneously with those species in which the intercoxal process is triangular, the hind coxæ being widely separated as in *helvola*, the process broad and truncate.

Occurs over a great extent of the Atlantic and Gulf region.

E. integra n. sp.—Oblong oval, rufo-testaceous, slightly shining, sparsely clothed with fulvous pubescence. Head moderately densely punctate. Antennæ pale rufous, club darker. Thorax rather less than twice as wide as long, base wider than apex, sides moderately arcuate, near the base obliquely narrowed and slightly sinuate, hind angles acute, moderately prominent, margin moderately explanate, slightly reflexed, apex moderately emarginate, base slightly sinuate on each side, surface moderately densely punctulate. Elytra oblong oval, one-third longer than wide, sides feebly arcuate and slightly narrowed to tip, margin narrowly reflexed, apices conjointly rounded, suture slightly dehiscent at tip, surface moderately densely punctulate. Body beneath and femora moderately densely punctulate. Intercoxal process of abdomen triangular. Length .12—.14 inch; 3—3.5 mm.

The sexual characters of the male are as in the preceding species, but the sinuation of the middle tibia of the male and the inward prolongation of the tip are feeble.

The form of the elytral tip, the absence of truncation, occurs in but few species in the entire genus, the elytra are in fact so complete that merely the tip of the pygidium is exposed.

Specimens are before me from Fort Whipple, Arizona, collected by Dr. Palmer, others from Colorado, by Morrison.

E. ambigua Mann.—Oblong oval, rufo-testaceous, elytra often clouded with fuscous, surface slightly shining, sparsely pubescent. Head sparsely punctulate. Antennæ rufous, club darker, funiculus as in *monogama*. Thorax nearly twice as wide as long, apex feebly emarginate, base a little wider than apex, broadly arcuate at middle, sides moderately arcuate, near the base obliquely narrowing, margin explanate and slightly reflexed, hind angles rectangular, surface sparsely punctulate. Elytra oblong oval, gradually narrowed to apex, one-half longer than wide at base, margin very narrowly reflexed, obsolete near the tip, surface finely and rather sparsely punctulate. Body beneath sparsely punctulate, abdomen more evidently, prothoracic side pieces smooth. Femora sparsely punctulate. Length .15 inch; 3.75 mm.

The sexual characters are as in *integra* but better marked, the sinuation of the middle tibia of the male being stronger and the inward prolongation of the tip greater.

The elytra are prolonged rather obliquely and there is but little separation at the tip, so that the abdomen is completely concealed. The sculpture is finer than in *integra* and there is no trace of sinuation of the side margin of the thorax, merely an oblique narrowing.

Occurs from Alaska to California.

E. Eriehsonii Reitter.—Oblong oval, pale luteous, moderately shining, sparsely clothed with fulvous pubescence. Head sparsely punctate. Antennæ pale luteous, formed as in *monogama*. Thorax less than twice as wide as long, slightly narrowed in front, apex feebly emarginate, base feebly sinuate on each side, sides feebly arcuate and subparallel behind, hind angles rectangular, margin feebly depressed, slightly reflexed, surface moderately densely and rather coarsely punctate. Elytra one-third longer than wide, sides feebly arcuate and slightly narrower to apex, tips truncate, margin narrowly reflexed, disc subdepressed, surface moderately densely punctate. Thorax beneath comparatively smooth, body and abdomen rather coarsely and densely punctate. Femora rather coarsely but sparsely punctate. Intercoxal process triangular acute. Length .10—.12 inch; 2.5—3 mm.

The sexual characters are as in *Hornii*, the sinuation of the middle tibia of the male being rather deep and the inward prolongation of the tip well marked.

For a type of this species I am indebted to Mr. Reitter, through the kind intercession of Dr. C. A. Dohrn.

Occurs from Canada to Georgia, and is not rare. It has been confounded with *labilis* Er., from which the sexual characters of the male are the only ones to be relied on to distinguish it.

E. rufida Mels.—Oblong oval, rufo-testaceous, moderately shining, sparsely clothed with fulvous pubescence. Head densely and moderately coarsely punctured. Antennæ pale rufous, club slightly **darker**, joints proportioned as in *monogama*. Thorax less than twice as wide **as long**, a little narrower at apex than base, apex feebly emarginate, base very feebly sinuate on each side, sides moderately arcuate, narrowed obliquely for a very short distance in front of base but not sinuate, hind angles rectangular, margin moderately widely explanate and very slightly reflexed, surface densely punctured. Elytra one-half longer than wide, sides parallel in front, slightly arcuately narrowing at apical third, margin narrowly reflexed, apex truncate, surface densely punctulate. Prothorax comparatively smooth beneath, body and abdomen densely punctured. Femora sparsely punctulate. Intercoxal process acute. Length .14—.16 inch; 3.5—4 mm.

The male has the sexual characters of the middle tibia better marked than any other species in our fauna, the inward prolongation at the tip being so well developed as to be really a decided deformity.

The specimens before me have all been collected in Pennsylvania.

E. corticina Erichs.—Oblong oval, rufo-testaceous, disc of thorax and elytra clouded with darker color, sparsely clothed with fulvous pubescence. Head sparsely punctured, frontal impression divided, moderately deep. Antennæ rufo-testaceous, club somewhat darker, structure as in *monogama*. Thorax one-half wider than long, apex slightly narrower than base, sides rather strongly arcuate, near the base sinuate, hind angles acute, slightly prominent, margin narrowly reflexed, disc at middle piceo-rufous, surface moderately densely punctulate. Elytra one-third longer than wide, sides feebly arcuate and slightly narrower towards the tip which is truncate, margin narrowly reflexed, surface moderately densely punctulate, disc clouded with fuscous. Body beneath piceo-rufous, moderately punctulate. Legs paler, femora sparsely punctulate. Intercoxal process triangular acute. Length .14 inch; 3.5 mm.

The middle tibiæ of the male are moderately strongly sinuate within, and the apex prolonged inwards but less than in *rufida*.

The elytra are usually clouded without any attempt at design, some specimens however have the disc fuscous with a large oval apical spot paler, a smaller near the humeri and also the suture and margin paler. It has a superficial resemblance to *immunda*, but may be known by the sexual characters.

Occurs especially in the Gulf States.

E. immunda Sturm.—Oblong oval, depressed, moderately shining, sparsely pubescent, color variable. Head moderately densely punctured. Antennæ pale, club piceous, structure as in *monogama*. Thorax twice as wide as long, narrower in front than base, apex feebly emarginate, base very feebly sinuate on each side, sides moderately arcuate, posteriorly obliquely but very feebly narrowed, hind angles rectangular, margin moderately explanate and feebly reflexed, surface moderately densely punctured. Elytra one-fourth longer than wide, sides feebly arcuate and slightly narrowing to apex which is obtusely truncate, margin rather wide and very distinctly reflexed. Body beneath rather densely and coarsely punctate. Length .12—.14 inch: 3 – 3.5 mm.

The male has the middle tibia sinuate within near the tip and very feebly prolonged inwards. This character is so feeble as to require care in observation.

The color of the specimens is variable, some being entirely pale or fulvous, others have the middle of the thorax fuscous and the sides of the elytra darker, the dark color forming a space exterior to a line drawn from the humeri to the suture at apex. The variety *flavomaculata* is piceous, the thoracic and elytral margins paler, the disc of each elytron with two oval, pale spots.

I have seen several types sent by Mäklin, one of which (that sent me by Dr. Dohrn of Stettin), enabled Mr. Reitter to fix the synonymy with *immunda*.

Occurs from Alaska to Massachusetts.

E. adumbrata Mann.—This species so closely resembles the preceding that I merely give the following distinctive characters. Thorax posteriorly distinctly sinuate, the hind angles acute and slightly prominent. Elytra very narrowly margined, margin feebly reflexed, apices rotundato-truncate. Length .12 inch; 3 mm.

The male has a form of middle tibia similar to the next species. I have however seen the other sex only.

Occurs in Alaska.

The four species with very feeble development of sexual characters although very closely allied are readily distinguished in nature; *fulvescens* has the sides of the thorax rounded near the base, and the margin not at all explanate; *avara* has the antennæ entirely pale and the sides of the thorax distinctly sinuate near the hind angles; *immunda* and *adumbrata* have the antennal club piceous, the former has the sides of the thorax very distinctly sinuate near the hind angles but the elytral margin is very narrow, the latter species has the sides obliquely narrowed posteriorly and the elytral margin rather wide.

E. avara Rand.—Elongate oval, rufo-testaceous, moderately shining, sparsely pubescent. Head sparsely punctate. Antennæ as in *corticina*. Thorax one-half wider than long, slightly narrower in front than at base, sides feebly arcuate, slightly obliquely narrowed posteriorly, hind angles rectangular, margin reflexed, disc moderately densely punctate. Elytra one-half wider than long, sides feebly arcuate and gradually narrowed posteriorly, apex truncate, margin reflexed, disc moderately densely punctate and often with three indistinct fuscous spots on each. Body beneath and legs colored as above, moderately densely punctate. Intercoxal process triangular acute. Length .12—.14 inch; 3—3.5 mm.

The male has the same sinuate middle tibia as in the preceding species but very much less marked, so that without a careful observation of the tibia extended it might be supposed to be simple. In this respect it differs notably from *corticina*, although there are other characters, such as the less arcuate sides of the thorax and less prominence of the hind angles and usually smaller size, more elongate and depressed form.

Occurs all over the United States and Canada, and from its wide distribution may be an introduced species, but from the published descriptions I have not been able to identify it satisfactorily.

E. fulvescens n. sp.—Oblong oval, fulvous, moderately shining, sparsely pubescent. Head sparsely punctate, frontal impression moderately deep. Antennæ fulvous, formed as in *monogama*. Thorax less than twice as wide as long, apex narrower than base, sides feebly arcuate, hind angles rectangular, base distinctly sinuate on each side, margin very narrowly reflexed, surface moderately densely punctulate. Elytra one-fourth longer than wide, sides feebly arcuate and slightly narrowed posteriorly, apex truncate, margin narrowly reflexed, surface punctured like the thorax. Body beneath moderately densely punctate, femora sparsely and finely punctulate. Length .12—.14 inch : 3—3.5 mm.

The middle tibiæ of the male are stouter than the posterior, somewhat sinuate within and thickened at tip, without however having the abrupt dilatation so often seen. Superficially the species greatly resembles *Erichsonii* of this group and *labilis* of the following, from both of which it differs by its larger size and less distinct punctuation, the former species having the middle tibiæ of the male suddenly dilated at tip, while the latter species has absolutely simple tibiæ.

All the specimens I have seen were collected by Mr. Johnson Pettit, at Grimsby, Canada.

E. linearis Mäkl.—Elongate, parallel, piceo-rufous, subopaque, sparsely pubescent. Head sparsely obsoletely punctulate. Antennæ rufous, joints 6 -7—8 small and very short. Thorax one-third wider than long, very little wider at base than apex, sides feebly arcuate, margin very narrowly reflexed, apex feebly emarginate, base truncate, hind angles obtusely rectangular, disc subopaque, very obsoletely finely punctate. Elytra rufous clouded with piceous, parallel, one-half longer than wide, margin very narrowly reflexed, apex rotundato-truncate, disc sculptured like the thorax. Body beneath darker than above, sparsely punctate. Legs rufo-testaceous, femora very sparsely finely punctate. Length .14 inch; 3.5 mm.

The middle tibiæ of the male are sinuate within near the tip and dilated inwards.

This species may be known from any in our fauna, except the next two, by its elongate parallel form, and from these by the opaque surface and form of thorax.

Occurs from Alaska to British Columbia.

E. truncatella Mann.—Elongate, parallel, piceo-testaceous or nearly black, sparsely pubescent, moderately shining. Head sparsely punctate. Antennæ rufous, club darker, funicle as in *monogama*. Thorax one-third wider than long, very little narrower in front, sides feebly arcuate and at posterior third obliquely narrowed, hind angles subrectangular, apex feebly emarginate, base truncate, margin narrowly explanate, more widely posteriorly and very slightly reflexed, surface densely punctate. Elytra parallel, slightly narrowed near the apex which is obtusely truncate, margin narrowly reflexed, disc slightly depressed, surface less densely punctured than the elytra. Body beneath moderately densely punctate. Femora sparsely punctulate. Length .10—.12 inch; 2.5—3 mm.

The sexual characters are as in *linearis*.

This species has a wide distribution and is found in Canada, Colorado, California, Oregon, and northward to Alaska. It varies in color and slightly in elongation, and resembles somewhat the next species.

E. planulata Erichs.—Elongate, rufo-piceous, moderately shining, sparsely pubescent. Head sparsely punctulate. Antennæ extending very little beyond the middle of the thorax, rufous, club piceous, joint 3 moderately elongate, 4—8 short. Thorax one-third wider than long, apex slightly narrower than base and feebly emarginate, sides moderately arcuate, very slightly narrowing at the base, margin moderately explanate but not reflexed, hind angles rectangular, base truncate, surface moderately densely punctulate. Elytra nearly one-half longer than wide, slightly narrowed toward the tip which is rotundato-truncate, margin narrowly reflexed, surface punctured like the thorax. Body beneath with moderately dense punctures coarser than those of the upper surface. Femora sparsely punctulate. Length .10—.12 inch; 2.5—3 mm.

The sexual characters are as in *truncatella*.

This species resembles *truncatella* but the sides of the thorax are not obliquely narrowed posteriorly. The antennæ are also shorter and differently formed.

All the specimens before me are from Alaska.

GROUP II.

In this group, which contains but few species, the tibiæ present no sexual characters whatever. Here also we have species with the posterior coxæ widely separated, and one (*peltoides*), in which the posterior femur of the male is very obtusely subangulate near the tip.

The species are as follows :

Intercoxal process broad, obtuse.
  Elytra narrowly margined. Posterior femora ♂ simple.................**ovata.**
  Elytra widely margined. Posterior femora ♂ obtusely subangulate.
                                                peltoides.
Intercoxal process triangular, more or less acute.
  Last joint of antennæ larger than the preceding.........................**æstiva.**
  Last joint of antennæ narrower and smaller than the preceding.
    Elytra rounded or truncate at tip.
      Thoracic margin rather narrowly explanate, hind angles distinct.
        Thorax regularly arcuately narrowed from base to apex........**labilis.**
        Thorax widest in front of middle............................**umbrosa.**
      Thoracic margin widely explanate, hind angles obtuse...**obtusicollis.**
    Elytra conjointly emarginate at tip.
      Margins of thorax and elytra widely reflexed.............**scaphoides.**

E. ovata n. sp.—Oval, piceous, moderately shining, sparsely clothed with short greyish pubescence. Head piceo-rufous, moderately densely punctulate. Antennæ rufous, club piceous, structure as in *monogama*. Thorax twice as wide as long, apex narrower than base and deeply emarginate, sides strongly arcuate, suddenly sinuate posteriorly, hind angles rectangular and slightly prominent, margin widely explanate and moderately reflexed, base on each side sinuate, surface piceo-rufous, moderately densely punctate. Elytra piceous, margin paler, very little longer than wide at base, sides arcuate and gradually narrowing to the apices which are conjointly rounded, margin narrowly reflexed, surface moderately densely punctate. Body beneath densely punctured. Legs piceous, femora moderately densely punctate. Intercoxal process broadly oval. Length .10—.12 inch ; 2.5—3 mm.

The middle tibiæ of the male are absolutely simple and not stouter than the corresponding portions of the female.

This species might be mistaken for a diminutive *helvola*, but besides its smaller size the sides of the thorax more suddenly sinuate posteriorly, the apices of the elytra not truncate and the sexual characters of the male will serve to disinguish it.

Occurs in Michigan, (Schwarz), Canada, (Pettit), and California, (Crotch).

E. peltoides n. sp.—Rather broadly oval, piceous, elytra maculate, moderately shining, very sparsely pubescent. Head piceo-testaceous, sparsely punctate. Antennæ rufous, club darker, structure as in *monogama*. Thorax twice as wide as long, narrower in front, apex deeply emarginate, base feebly sinuate on each side, sides rather strongly arcuate, at basal third subparallel and feebly sinuate, hind angles rectangular, margin broadly explanate and moderately reflexed, disc convex rather sparsely punctate, color piceous, margin broadly median line narrowly testaceous. Elytra nearly as wide as long, sides gradually arcuately narrowing, margin broadly explanate and moderately reflexed, apex rotundato-truncate, disc moderately convex, punctured like the thorax, color piceous, margin and four oval, badly defined paler spots on each side paler. Body beneath paler than above, rather sparsely and finely punctate. Intercoxal process moderately broad, obtuse at tip. Length .10 inch; 2.5 mm.

The tibiæ of the male are all simple as in the female, the posterior femora are however obtusely subangulate near the tip.

In form this species resembles *helvola*, and is equally widely margined.

Occurs in Michigan, (Schwarz), also in Maryland.

E. æstiva Linn.—Oval, slightly oblong, rufo-testaceous, moderately shining, sparsely pubescent. Head densely punctate. Antennæ as in *monogama*, pale rufous. Thorax nearly twice as wide as long, apex very feebly emarginate and narrower than the base which is very feebly sinuate on each side, sides moderately arcuate, hind angles obtusely rectangular, margin narrowly explanate and slightly reflexed, disc moderately convex and with a slight depression near the hind angles, surface moderately densely punctured. Elytra one-fourth longer than wide, sides slightly arcuate and gradually narrowed to apices which are separately rounded, margin narrowly reflexed, disc moderately convex, a little less densely punctured than the thorax. Body beneath rather densely punctured, more coarsely than the upper surface. Intercoxal process acutely oval in front. Length .12—.14 inch; 3—3.5 mm.

The tibiæ are simple and similar in the two sexes.

The terminal joint of the antennal club is somewhat quadrangular and nearly equal in size to the two preceding joints together, and in the female rather larger than the male. This will distinguish this species from any other in our fauna.

Occurs in Alaska.

E. labilis Erichs.—Oval, rufo-testaceous, moderately shining, sparsely pubescent. Head moderately densely and coarsely punctured. Antennæ pale, formed as in *monogama*. Thorax twice as wide as long, apex narrower than base and feebly emarginate, sides regularly arcuate and gradually narrowing from base to apex, margin narrowly reflexed, hind angles rectangular, surface rather coarsely and moderately densely punctured. Elytra one-third longer than wide, sides feebly arcuate and slightly narrowing posteriorly, apex truncate, margin narrowly reflexed, surface punctured similarly to the thorax. Body beneath moderately densely punctulate. Intercoxal process triangular acute. Length .08—.10 inch; 2—2.5 mm.

The tibiæ are simple and similar in the two sexes.

Although always smaller this species resembles two already described, *Erichsonii* and *fulvescens*, and excepting size I know of no means of distinguishing with certainty the females. The male characters are however quite distinct as will be seen by reference to these species.

Occurs from Michigan to Georgia, and is rather common.

E. umbrosa n. sp.—Oval, slightly oblong, rufo-testaceous, moderately shining, sparsely pubescent. Head coarsely punctured, frontal impression moderately deep. Antennæ pale, formed as in *monogama*. Thorax less than twice as wide as long, apex feebly emarginate, slightly narrower than the base which is distinctly sinuate on each side, sides feebly arcuate and slightly narrower at base than at middle, hind angles rectangular, margin narrowly reflexed, surface rather coarsely and moderately densely punctured. Elytra one-fourth longer than wide, slightly narrower posteriorly, sides feebly arcuate, margin narrowly reflexed, apex truncate, surface clouded with fuscous, punctured similarly to the thorax. Body beneath moderately densely punctate. Intercoxal process triangular acute. Length .14 inch; 3.5 mm.

Sexual characters as in *labilis*.

This species resembles a large *labilis*, but the thorax is narrower at base than at middle, the surface more coarsely punctured and the elytra clouded with fuscous, so that an oval pale intra-humeral spot and another subapical are indicated.

Two specimens, Fort Cobb, Indian Territory.

E. obtusicollis Reitter.—Ovate, rufo-testaceous, feebly shining, sparsely pubescent. Head moderately densely punctate. Antennæ pale, club fuscous. Thorax rather more than twice as wide as long, apex feebly emarginate, narrower than the base which is feebly sinuate on each side, sides feebly arcuate, hind angles obtusely rounded, margin rather widely explanate and slightly reflexed. Elytra one-fourth longer than wide, slightly narrowed toward apex which is rotundato-truncate, margin rather narrowly reflexed, surface (also the thorax), moderately densely punctate. Body beneath moderately densely punctate. Length .10 inch; 2.5 mm.

The male has no sexual characters excepting the additional dorsal segment. The elytra are obliquely infuscate at the sides.

I have seen only Mr. Reitter's type, which privilege I owe to the great kindness of Mr. Chevrolat, through the intercession of M. Sallé.

Its habitat is vaguely stated Am. Bor., and may not be from our country.

E. scaphoides n. sp.—Elongate oval, rufo-testaceous, moderately shining, sparsely pubescent. Head moderately densely punctate. Antennæ rufous, formed as in *monogama*. Thorax one-third wider than long, slightly narrower in front, apex deeply emarginate, base truncate, sides very feebly arcuate, hind angles rectangular, margin widely explanate and broadly reflexed, surface moderately densely punctate. Elytra one-third longer than wide, slightly narrower posteriorly, apices conjointly emarginate, margin rather widely explanate and broadly reflexed, surface punctured as the thorax. Body beneath piceous, not densely punctate. Legs pale. Intercoxal process triangular acute. Length .12 inch; 3 mm.

Sexual characters as in *labilis*.

This is one of the most peculiar species in our fauna, if it really belongs to the genus. I feel unwilling with the material before me to separate it, in fact there is no character in which it differs from *Epuraea*, although I suspect that the tarsi are not dilated, there is however but one tarsal joint remaining in the specimen in my cabinet, although I have seen two others equally mutilated. It resembles a miniature *Embaphion* with the elytra conjointly emarginate.

Collected in Colorado, by H. K. Morrison.

GROUP III.

This group contains but one small species in which the posterior tibiæ of the male are slender at the basal two-fifths, while the apical portion is rather suddenly twice as wide as it. (Pl. III, fig. 20).

E. luteola Erichs.—Oval, slightly oblong, fulvo-testaceous, moderately shining, sparsely pubescent. Head sparsely punctulate. Antennæ pale, club darker, formed as in *monogama*. Thorax nearly twice as wide as long, narrowed in front, apex feebly emarginate, base truncate, sides feebly arcuate, hind angles rectangular, margin very narrowly reflexed, surface not densely punctate. Elytra very little longer than wide, slightly narrowed posteriorly, apex truncate, margin very narrowly reflexed, disc moderately convex punctured like the thorax. Body beneath rather finely and sparsely punctulate. Length .08—.09 inch; 2—2.25 mm.

The middle tibiæ are simple in the two sexes. The posterior tibiæ of the male are slightly arcuate, the basal half slender, the apical half rather suddenly broader although not much dilated. Mr. Crotch's reference of this species to *Dadopora* Thoms., associating it with *decemguttata* is entirely erroneous.

This species is one of the smallest in our fauna, and the females can be distinguished from those of *labilis* by the sparser punctuation and more narrowly reflexed margin, they otherwise greatly resemble that species.

In distribution this species appears to be becoming cosmopolitan. Originally occurring in our Gulf States and Cuba, it has spread to Europe, (Reiche), and Ceylon, (Murray).

Mr. Reitter has placed this species in a genus of his own creation, *Haptoncura*, the characters of which seem to me entirely too feeble to adopt.

In addition to the foregoing species, Mr. Reitter describes from our fauna :

E. macrophthalma Reitter.—Elongata, subdepressa, subnitida, levissime punctulata, tenuiter puberula, testaceo-ferruginea, antice attenuata; oculis grandibus, nigris, thorace transverso, antice et apice subtruncato, lateribus levissime rotundatis, antice valde angustatis, vix marginato-reflexis; elytris thorace paulo latioribus, elongatis, subparallelïs, apice truncatïs, pygidium ex parte obtegente; unguiculi basi dentati. Long. 3.4 mm, (.14 inch).

I have not seen anything corresponding with this. The locality is in all probability erroneous.

Mr. Reitter has since placed this in a new genus, *Micruria*, with other species.

E. flavescens Reitter, cited as having been collected in Chicago, is from Chiapas. Mr. Sallé having kindly examined the type in Chevrolat's cabinet.

I would here call the attention of those having occasion to use Mr. Reitter's descriptions, that what everybody else calls the base of the thorax, he calls the apex. I have several times been confused by this form of expression.

NITIDULA Fab.

Antennæ eleven-jointed, terminated by a suddenly formed club of three joints, received in grooves beneath and in front of the eyes. Labrum feebly emarginate. Maxillary palpi rather slender, the terminal joint longest, subacute at tip. Prosternum dilated at tip, not prolonged. Tarsi feebly dilated, the third joint feebly emarginate. Abdominal segments 2—5 equal, the first very little longer. Males without accessory segment.

This genus is allied closely to *Epuraca* but differs in the form of the labrum, somewhat also in the length of the abdominal segments, the rather less dilated tarsi and the sexual character.

Three species are known in our fauna, briefly distinguished as follows :

Thorax coarsely and moderately densely punctured.
    Piceous, each elytron with discal rufous spot............................**bipustulata.**
    Piceous, elytra uniform...**rufipes.**
Thorax sparsely and rather finely punctured.
    Elytra variable, often ornate with irregular paler spots..................**ziczac.**

N. bipustulata Linn.—Oval, feebly convex, piceous, finely pubescent, each elytron with rufous spot, legs rufous. Head coarsely punctured. Thorax twice as wide at base as long, apex a little broader than the length, sides moderately arcuate, margin moderately explanate, hind angles nearly rectangular, surface rather coarsely and moderately densely punctured. Elytra longer than wide conjointly, rather sparsely and finely punctured, finely pubescent. Pygidium densely punctured. Body beneath rather coarsely and densely punctured. Length .16—.20 inch; 5—6 mm.

I am unable to detect any sexual differences, except that the last ventral of male is a little less arcuate at apex.

Originally described from Europe, this species is now found everywhere in the Atlantic and Gulf States.

N. rufipes Linn.—Oval, slightly oblong, piceous, subopaque, pubescent, antennæ (except club), and legs rufous. Thorax less than twice as wide as long, apex but little narrower than base, sides moderately arcuate, margin narrowly explanate, surface densely and coarsely punctured. Length .14—.16 inch: 3.5—4 mm.

This species is closely allied to the preceding but is without elytral spot, of a little more elongate form, the thorax much less narrowed in front and the sides less explanate.

Introduced from Europe into the Eastern States and Canada.

N. ziczac Say.—Oblong oval, piceous, subopaque, pubescent, elytra with basal spots and a median sigmoid band testaceous. Head moderately finely not densely punctured. Thorax a little less than twice as wide as long, apex a little narrower than the base, sides feebly arcuate, margin very feebly explanate, surface sparsely and rather finely punctured. Elytra finely not densely punctured. Length .12—.20 inch; 3—5 mm.

The above characters sufficiently represent the typical form from which we have several variations.

var. **uniguttata** Mels.—This is the form in which the median portion of the sigmoid band alone remains.

var. **humeralis** Lec.—Here the sigmoid band disappears and the juxta-humeral spot alone remains.

var. **inornata.**—These are entirely immaculate and of a pale piceous color.

In the fully colored specimens the pubescence is not uniformly brown as in the preceding species but is intermixed with grey, and the elytral spots are covered with grey pubescence, and a vitta of similar color starts at the humerus and crosses the elytra in front of the tip. The pubescence is also coarser than in the two preceding.

The differences between this species and the preceding are so evident as to require no special mention. It will however be noticed that the tarsi are a little less dilated.

Occurs everywhere in the United States. including the Pacific Coast and also in Canada.

STELIDOTA Erichs.

Labrum bilobed. Mandibles feebly bidentate at apex, the terminal cusp simple not bifid. Antennæ with an abrupt club, grooves sub-ocular, moderately deep, parallel. Tarsi dilated.

The males have an additional segment which varies in distinctness in the species, being nearly as evident in *octomaculata* as in the males of *Epuraea*, while in the other two species the segment is quite as feebly developed as in *Phenolia*. *S. geminata* ♂ has in addition the middle and posterior tibiæ dilated in a manner similar to the posterior tibiæ of *Epuraea luteola*. (Pl. III, fig. 22).

Our species are distinguished as follows :

Thorax at apex deeply emarginate, base distinctly bisinuate, margin broad and deplanate.
Thorax arcuately narrowed from base to apex, broadest at base...**geminata.**
Thorax with sides more arcuate at base, so that the thorax is narrower at base than a little in front..**octomaculata.**
Thorax at apex feebly emarginate, base truncate, margin narrow and not deplanate. Broadest at base...**strigosa.**

S. geminata Say.—Oval, narrower posteriorly, piceous or rufo-piceous, margins paler, elytra maculate with paler spots. Head coarsely and moderately deeply punctured. Thorax twice as wide as long, narrower in front, apex deeply emarginate, base bisinuate, sides regularly arcuate from base to apex, margin broad, deplanate, hind angles rectangular, disc moderately convex, coarsely and densely punctured. Elytra as wide at base as the thorax, arcuately narrowed to apex, margin moderately reflexed, disc obsoletely subcostate, the costæ with a single row of fine punctures each bearing a short hair, the grooves between the costæ closely punctured with a catenulate appearance. Body beneath moderately densely punctured. Length .08—.10 inch ; 2—2.5 mm.

Male.—Middle and posterior tibiæ distinctly arcuate, the former suddenly dilated in its distal half, the latter in the distal third. Sexual segment small.

Female.—Tibiæ simple, not arcuate.

Mr. Reitter has described a *S. biseriata*, a type of which was procured through the kindness of Dr. Dohrn, of Stettin. It does not differ specifically from *geminata*.

Occurs in the Middle and Southern Atlantic States.

S. octomaculata Say.—Oval, narrower posteriorly, piceous or rufo-piceous, elytra variably maculate with paler spots. Thorax twice as wide as long, narrower in front, apex deeply emarginate, base bisinuate, sides arcuate, slightly coarctate at base, hind angles rectangular, margin broad, moderately deplanate. Elytra as in *geminata*, surface not subcostate, but with the rows of fine hair-bearing punctures between which are rows of large, round, shallow punctures. Body beneath coarsely and densely punctured. Length .08—.10 inch ; 2—2.5 mm.

The males have quite a distinct sexual segment. The tibiæ show no peculiarities, but occasional males are met with in which the tooth above the oblique emargination of the posterior tibiæ is a little more evident.

Occurs from the New England States to Florida.

S. strigosa Schönherr.—Oval, narrower posteriorly, piceous, elytra indistinctly maculate. Thorax nearly twice as wide as long, narrowed in front, sides arcuate, more strongly toward the front, apex feebly emarginate, base truncate, hind angles rectangular, margin very narrow not deplanate, disc moderately convex, punctures rather dense, coarse and substrigose. Elytra not subcostate, but with the series of small hair-bearing punctures and between them the usual row of coarse closely placed punctures. Body beneath densely punctured. Length .06—.08 inch ; 1.5—2 mm.

This species is the smallest of the series, and is known by the form of the thorax and the narrow margin. The males have the usual sexual segment, and the posterior tibiæ at tip are a very little more dilated than in the female.

Occurs in South Carolina, Georgia and Florida.

PROMETOPIA Erichs.

Mentum large, entirely closing the mouth beneath. Labrum nearly semicircular. Mandibles prominent, bifid at tip. Antennal grooves moderately deep, slightly convergent. Antennæ slender, first joint stout, third very long, club elongate oval. Front not lobed at the sides. Thorax deeply emarginate in front, sides explanate. Prosternum flat, tip not prolonged. Tarsi very feebly dilated.

The males have an additional segment visible only beneath, received in a slight emargination of the fifth ventral and similar to that of *Colastus*.

One species only occurs in our fauna.

P. sexmaculata Say.—Broadly oval, depressed, piceous, margins paler. Head finely punctulate. Thorax twice as wide as long, narrower in front, apex deeply emarginate, base truncate, sides feebly arcuate, hind angles rectangular, margins explanate, disc feebly convex not densely punctate with coarse and fine punctures intermixed. Elytra as wide as long ♂, or longer than wide ♀, surface sparsely coarsely punctate, margins pale, disc piceous with an irregular humeral band and a spot at apical third paler. Body beneath paler than above, sparsely punctate. Length .20—.24 inch: 5—6 mm.

The males are always broader than the females, and have an additional segment as in *Colastus*.

Occurs from the Middle States to Missouri and Texas.

PHENOLIA Erichs.

Labrum feebly bilobed. Front not lobed over the insertion of the antennæ. Antennæ terminated by an abrupt club, first joint not auriculate, grooves moderately deep situated under the eye, not convergent. Mandibles bifid at tip, not dentate within. Tarsi not dilated.

The males have a small additional segment visible only beneath as in *Colastus*.

This genus has been united with *Soronia* by Mr. E. Reitter, but the differences as far as our species is concerned seems not to warrant this conclusion. The absence of the supra-antennal lobe of the front, together with the simpler form of the first joint of the antennæ, it being merely thickened, not auriculate, are sufficient in this family to retain *Phenolia* as distinct. The mandibles are, moreover, bifid at tip and not simple, resembling in this respect *Prometopia*.

P. grossa Fab.—Piceous, feebly shining, elongate oval, elytra maculate with paler spots. Head coarsely punctured, front transversely impressed. Thorax twice as wide as long, apex a little narrower than base, sides moderately arcuate, posteriorly distinctly sinuate, hind angles subacute, apex deeply emarginate, base feebly bisinuate, margin explanate, feebly reflexed, disc vaguely impressed each side of middle, surface coarsely and moderately densely punctate. Elytra as wide as the thorax, sutural angle slightly rounded, disc feebly subcostate, each ridge with a row of fine punctures bearing a short hair, intervals vaguely triseriately punctate, color piceous maculate with paler spots, one each side of scutellum, an oblique row of three spots, the outer humeral the inner at the middle of the suture, behind this row another similar one of three spots. Body beneath densely punctate, the abdomen less so than the metasternum. Length .24—.34 inch; 6—8.5 mm.

This is our largest Nitidulide with the exception of an Ips.

Occurs from Canada to Texas.

OMOSITA Erichs.

Labrum entire. Front not lobed at the sides. Antennal grooves moderately deep, feebly convergent beneath. Point of prosternum not prolonged. Tarsi moderately dilated.

There is no additional segment in the males.

Two species occur in our fauna, identical with those of Europe, but probably equally native to our continent and not introduced. They are so abundant and well known that no detailed description need be given.

O. colon Linn.—Piceous, elytra spotted with testaceous, a large apical testaceous space enclosing on each side a small piceous spot. Length .10—.14 inch; 2.5—3.5 mm.

Eastern United States and Europe.

O. discoidea Fab.—Somewhat more elongate than the preceding, similarly colored except that the large pale space is basal. Length .10—.16 inch; 2.5—4 mm.

Occurs in Europe and in the Pacific States, extending as far east as Colorado.

SORONIA Erichs.

Labrum emarginate or feebly bilobed. Mandibles with an acute cusp behind the tip, apex simple not bifid. Front distinctly lobed over the insertion of the antennæ. Antennæ terminated by the usual club, received in grooves under the eyes, either parallel or slightly convergent, first joint always auriculate but variably in extent. Tarsi extremely feebly dilated.

The males are as in *Phenolia*.

Under this head Mr. Reitter has united *Soronia*, *Lobiopa* and *Phenolia*. I fully agree with him as to the first two but not the last, giving my reasons under that genus for the disagreement. I am, however, disposed to go a step further and suppress *Amphotis*, as there does not appear to be any valid reason for retaining it as distinct.

The antennal groove is beneath the eye which forms its upper limit, the lower or inner limit is formed by a ridge or plate which is nearly continuous with the edge of the mandible. This plate is more perfectly developed in the species heretofore referred to *Amphotis*, least so in *Soronia*, so that by the partial imperfection of this plate posteriorly the antennal grooves converge posteriorly, while they appear absolutely parallel in *Amphotis*. This difference affords a means of dividing our species quite naturally.

Antennal grooves very decidedly convergent posteriorly.
    (Sides of thorax suddenly narrowed at base, the hind angles retracted within
    the humeral angles)..**grisea.**
    Sides of thorax very feebly sinuate at base, the hind angles not retracted,
    the base as wide as the base of the elytra.............................**guttulata.**
Antennal grooves parallel.
    Elytra not or merely apparently costate.................................**undulata.**
    Elytra distinctly costate.
        Thorax slightly coarctate at base, the explanate margin punctured; lateral
        angles of mentum prominent, acute...**Ulkei.**
        (Thorax broadest at base, hind angles rectangular, the explanate margin
        smooth; lateral angles of mentum rounded).................**marginata.**

Two European species are introduced into the table to show the relationship of our species with them. In *undulata* the antennal grooves are neither exactly parallel nor are they by any means convergent, the inner plate of which mention has been made is arcuate, so that if the insect is looked at directly from the front the grooves seem parallel, if from the rear they seem slightly convergent. *S. guttulata* by its narrower elytral margin approaches *Phenolia ;* it has the widest distribution of all the species.

S. guttulata Lec.—Piceous or somewhat paler, feebly shining, very sparsely pubescent, elongate oval. Head moderately densely finely punctured and with a sinuous impression. Antennæ rufous, third joint nearly as long as the two following united, club piceous. Thorax twice as wide as long, broadest at base, apex deeply emarginate, base feebly bisinuate, sides regularly arcuate, posteriorly feebly sinuate, hind angles subacute slightly dentiform, margin broadly explanate, disc moderately convex, a distinct median impression and on each side about four vague foveæ, surface moderately densely finely punctured to the extreme margin. Elytra at base as broad as the thorax, humeral angles slightly dentiform, margin moderately explanate, slightly reflexed, surface less densely and more finely punctured than the thorax, sparsely clothed with brownish pubescence with short pale semierect setæ in rows, distantly placed; color piceous, margin paler, disc with a common sinuous band slightly behind the middle, of pale testaceous color, a vague oblique band less pale than the preceding beginning at the humerus, and numerous small pale spots irregularly scattered. Body beneath moderately densely finely punctured, prosternum very sparsely punctured. Length .20 inch : 5 mm.

This species was placed by Crotch as a synonym of *S. grisea*, but it differs by its more elongate form and the shape of the thorax as indicated in the synoptic table. (Pl. III, figs. 8—9).

Occurs from Canada to Nevada, and is probably one of those northern transcontinental species whose habitat will be found from Maine to Oregon.

S. undulata Say.—Rather broadly oval, piceous, margins paler, elytra maculate, subopaque, sparsely pubescent. Head not densely punctulate, front semicircularly impressed. Thorax more than twice as wide as long at middle, narrower in front, apex deeply emarginate, base feebly bisinuate, sides moderately arcuate, near hind angles slightly narrowed, hind angles not prominent, surface moderately densely punctured at middle,' sparsely at the sides, disc more vaguely impressed than in *guttulata*, piceous with paler spots. Elytra slightly wider than the base of the thorax, the humeral angles feebly dentiform, surface a little more coarsely punctured than the thorax, the punctures on the margin much finer and sparser; margins pale, disc piceous with a postmedian ziczac band and numerous paler spots. Body beneath finely and sparsely punctulate. Length .16—.20 inch ; 4—5 mm.

As already remarked the antennal grooves are nearly parallel but the inner ridge slightly arcuate. The antennal club is less suddenly formed than in *guttulata*, the basal joint being triangular and not semicircular. The markings of this species are an almost exact reproduction of those of *S. grisea*, from which it differs in the form of the thorax, the present being slightly arcuately narrowed at base, the other suddenly obliquely narrowed.

Occurs from the Middle States to Utah.

S. Ulkei Lec.—Elongate oval, chestnut brown, opaque. Head densely punctured, front not impressed. Antennæ less elongate, third joint not as long as the two following united, club abrupt. Thorax twice as wide as the length at middle, narrowed in front, apex very deeply emarginate, base feebly bisinuate, sides moderately arcuate, hind angles rectangular, not dentiform, margin broadly explanate, not reflexed, disc not foveate, densely punctured, punctures at margin sparser. Elytra as wide at base as the thorax, humeral angles slightly dentiform, margin broad, moderately reflexed, disc moderately convex, with a sutural and fine feeble discal costæ which have fine punctures at their summits bearing short hairs, the intervals irregularly transversely coarsely punctured, margin more sparsely and less distinctly punctured. Body beneath densely punctured. Length .24—.28 inch ; 6—7 mm.

In two of the specimens before me the color is uniformly brown, in the third the elytra are indistinctly maculate as in *Phenolia grossa*.

Massachusetts, Delaware, District of Columbia.

THALYCRA Erichs.

Labrum feebly visible, bilobed. Front at middle prolonged, the sides parallel, truncate in front. Antennæ with abrupt three-jointed club, no antennal grooves distinctly defined. Mandibles simple at tip, a small tooth behind the apex. Prosternum elevated, subconical and slightly prolonged at tip, not laminiform, mesosternum not carinate. Anterior tibiæ triangularly dilated, the outer apical angle dentiform, middle and posterior spinulose externally and at tip. Anterior tarsi dilated, the middle a little broadened, the posterior slender. Claws simple. Elytra entire.

The males have a very distinct additional dorsal segment.

This genus differs from all our genera of the present tribe (excepting *Perthalycra*), by the absence of antennal grooves, and from the latter by the form of the anterior tibiæ and the tarsi. The structure of the prosternum is radically different from that of *Meligethes* and the mesosternum is without carina.

One species only is known in our fauna.

T. concolor Lec.—Oblong oval, rufo-ferruginous, moderately shining, sparsely pubescent. Head and thorax moderately densely punctate. Thorax twice as wide as long, narrower in front, base arcuate, apex feebly emarginate, sides feebly arcuate, margin very narrow, finely fimbriate, hind angles obtusely rectangular, disc convex. Elytra as broad as the thorax, about one-fourth longer than wide, sides and apex arcuate, surface as coarsely punctured as the thorax but less densely, the punctures becoming rapidly finer and finally near the apex obsolete. Prosternum very sparsely finely punctate. Mesosternum and abdomen coarsely and moderately densely punctate. Length .14 inch; 3.5 mm.

I have seen but one male specimen, collected by Dr. Leconte, on the north shore of Lake Superior.

PERTHALYCRA n. g.

Labrum moderately prominent, bilobed. Epistoma at middle slightly prolonged. Mandibles acute at tip, a small tooth behind the tip. Mentum transverse, longest at middle. Last joint of maxillary palpi conical obtuse, labial ovate, slightly compressed and truncate. Antennæ rather short, club broadly oval, three-jointed, last joint small, retracted, grooves very feebly marked, strongly convergent. Prosternum convex between the coxæ, the tip obtusely prolonged. Anterior tibiæ triangular, the apical angle prolonged, the apical margin posteriorly dentate, outer edge bidentate at middle, middle and posterior tibiæ strongly spinulose. Tarsi slender, the anterior dilated in the male only. Claws simple.

The males have an additional segment and the anterior tarsi dilated.

This genus as will be seen, is closely allied to *Thalycra*, but differs in the anterior tibiæ dentate externally and the anterior tarsi dilated in the male only. The antennal club although three-jointed in both sexes is much more distinctly so in the male, the terminal joint in the other sex being strongly retracted.

One species is known.

P. Murrayi n. sp.—Oblong oval, castaneous or piceous, feebly shining, sparsely pubescent. Head and thorax moderately densely and coarsely punctured. Thorax less than twice as wide as long, slightly narrower in front, apex feebly emarginate, base very feebly arcuate, sides moderately arcuate, narrowly margined, finely fimbriate, hind angles obtuse. Elytra as wide as the thorax, and more than twice as long, one-third longer than wide, sides very feebly arcuate, apex feebly truncate, surface less densely punctured than the thorax. Body beneath sparsely punctate. Length .12—.16 inch; 3—4 mm. (Pl. III, fig. 25).

The anterior tibiæ have the outer apical angle prolonged and bidentate, the posterior edge of the apical margin with three or four stout spines; the outer edge has two acute teeth near the middle. The middle tibiæ are furnished with stout spines arranged in a double series, two near the tip longer, the tip is also spinulose. The posterior tibia is like the middle.

This insect occurs from San Francisco northward to Oregon and Western Nevada. There is also a specimen in Dr. Leconte's cabinet labelled Georgia.

POCADIUS Erichs.

Labrum moderately prominent, bilobed. Front prolonged at middle, feebly emarginate. Antennal club oval, three-jointed, grooves deep and slightly convergent. Prosternum convex between the coxæ, tip with conical protuberance, mesosternum not carinate. Tibiæ rather slender, the outer apical angle of all spiniform, the middle and posterior ciliate externally and with a few spinules. Tarsi slender on all the feet, the claws simple.

The males have a small additional segment.

The simple tarsi will distinguish this genus from any other with the protuberant prosternum.

Two species occur in our fauna.

Thorax narrowly margined. Ferruginous.................................**helvolus.**
Thorax widely margined. Black, disc of elytra ferruginous...........**dorsalis.**

P. helvolus Erichs.—Broadly oval, robust, ferruginous, elytra sometimes darker at sides and apex, sparsely pubescent. Head coarsely irregularly punctured, front transversely impressed. Antennæ rufous. Thorax more than twice as wide as long, narrowed in front, apex emarginate, base arcuate, slightly sinuate each side, sides moderately arcuate, narrowly margined, disc convex, coarsely irregularly punctured. Elytra as wide as the thorax, a little longer than wide, sides moderately arcuate, apex rotundate truncate, sutural angle slightly dentiform, disc convex with ten rows of vaguely impressed punctures, the intervals very slightly convex, irregularly biseriately punctulate, each puncture with a short fulvous hair. Body beneath coarsely sparsely punctured. Length .12—.16 inch; 3—4 mm.

Mr. Reitter has described two species from our territory which are known to us as mere color varieties of *helvolus*. *P. infuscatus* has each elytron slightly darker at its middle. *P. limbatus* has the elytra darker at the sides, *breviusculus* is a small form found in the Gulf States. Through the kindness of Dr. Dohrn, I have seen the types of these species and find the first merely a stained specimen, the second a slight color variety.

Occurs in Pennsylvania, Kansas and Georgia.

P. dorsalis n. sp.—Broadly oval, subdepressed, black, shining, very sparsely pubescent, elytra with a large basal space rufous. Head coarsely sparsely punctured, front triangularly impressed. Antennæ piceous. Thorax more than twice as wide as long, narrowed in front, apex feebly emarginate, base arcuate at middle vaguely sinuate each side, sides moderately arcuate, margin distinctly but narrowly explanate, hind angles rectangular, disc moderately convex, coarsely but sparsely punctured. Elytra very little longer than wide, sides feebly arcuate, apices separately rounded, sutural angle not dentiform, disc subdepressed, with ten rows of closely placed, but feebly impressed quadrate punctures, intervals flat with a single series of fine punctures. Body beneath black, shining, sparsely punctured. Length .16 inch; 4 mm.

This species is less convex than *helvolus* and slightly more elongate, its sculpture is more distinct and regular and the pubescence less marked. The discal rufous space of the elytra occupies the basal two-thirds but does not attain the margin.

Two specimens, California, sent me by Mr. Ulke.

ORTHOPEPLUS n. g.

Labrum bilobed, but feebly. Mandibles acute at tip. Mentum and palpi as in *Epuraea*. Antennæ with an abrupt club, grooves broad, badly defined, convergent. Prosternum at tip feebly conically protuberant. Mesosternum depressed not carinate, middle coxæ narrowly separated. Tibiæ feebly broader at tip. Tarsi of the middle and posterior legs simple, the anterior dilated. Elytra truncate at tip. Surface glabrous.

The males have a distinct sexual segment.

I cannot place the species on which the above genus is founded, in any of the genera at present established. The form is that of the more elongate *Epuraeæ* such as *truncatella*, parallel and moderately convex. The thorax is nearly square and the head above concave, these give the species a peculiar appearance. The prosternum is elevated at tip and subconically protuberant, suggesting an affinity with *Thalycra* and *Pocadius*, with which there is otherwise very little resemblance. It may be called a glabrous *Epuraea* with protuberant prosternum with the anterior tarsi alone dilated.

O. quadricollis n. sp.—Elongate, parallel, piceo-rufous, elytra nearly black, moderately shining, glabrous. Head concave, minutely and sparsely punctulate, rufous. Antennæ rufous, club darker and longer than the funicle. Thorax quadrate, very slightly narrower posteriorly, apex feebly emarginate, sides feebly arcuate and narrowly margined, base slightly arcuate, disc feebly convex, anteriorly transversely flattened, rather finely punctulate, color rufous. Elytra parallel, very narrowly margined, apex obtusely truncate, disc with a feeble oblique impression from the humeri toward the suture, surface sparsely punctulate, punctures finer near the apex. Body beneath piceous, sparsely punctulate, abdomen more coarsely punctured and sparsely pubescent. Length .10 inch; 2.5 mm. (Pl. III, fig. 24).

The male has the small terminal abdominal segment.

One specimen, Colorado, (Morrison).

MELIGETHES Steph.

Labrum very feebly prominent. Antennæ with an abrupt three-jointed club, the grooves deep and nearly parallel. Point of prosternum free, overlapping the mesosternum. Elytra truncate at apex, pygidium exposed. Tarsi dilated, claws simple or dentate. Tibiæ serrate or finely denticulate. Last ventral segment with deeply impressed, semicircular line on each side, usually in great part concealed by the retraction of the segment.

There does not appear to be any additional segment in the male, nor any special sexual characters. The nearly concealed labrum, all the tarsi dilated, and the impressed line of the last ventral segment distinguish this genus from any other in our fauna. The species are extremely difficult to define, there appears to be a degree of variation in sculpture within specific limits which is very confusing.

The following table defines such as I have been able to separate satisfactorily.

Claws simple. Clypeus scarcely emarginate.
    Anterior tibiæ serrate, the middle emarginate externally................**sævus.**
    Anterior tibiæ finely denticulate, the middle simple.
        Thorax with the margin distinctly explanate.
            The explanate margin extending from base to apex.........**rufimanus.**
            The explanate margin not attaining the base......................**mutatus.**
        Thorax very narrowly margined, the margin not explanate..**seminulum.**
Claws toothed at base. Clypeus rather deeply emarginate.
    Anterior tibiæ coarsely serrate. Thoracic margin very narrow.....**pinguis.**

M. sævus Lec.—Oval, black, shining, very sparsely pubescent. Head moderately densely punctured. Antennæ piceous. Thorax a little less than twice as wide as long, narrowed in front, sides moderately arcuate, margin narrow, hind angles obtuse, disc convex, moderately densely punctate. Elytra a little longer than wide conjointly, surface a little more coarsely punctured than the thorax. Beneath black, not densely punctate. Anterior tibiæ serrate, middle tibiæ emarginate on the outer side near the tip and finely spinulose, posterior tibiæ dilated, finely spinulose. Length .08—.10 inch; 2—2.5 mm.

The claws are simple, the prosternum slightly broader behind the coxæ and rounded at tip. The front is extremely feebly emarginate, the angles distinct. Claws simple.

This species is one of the most easily known of any in our fauna. It is always black and never with any metallic lustre.

Occurs in Missouri and Kansas.

M. rufimanus Lec.—Oval, slightly oblong, black, thorax æneous, elytra blue, sparsely pubescent. Head æneous, moderately densely punctured. Antennæ piceous. Thorax twice as wide as long, narrower in front, sides moderately arcuate, margin from base to apex narrowly explanate, hind angles obtusely rectangular, disc convex, moderately densely punctured. Elytra one-fourth longer than wide, slightly narrowed to apex, surface rather finely and sparsely punctate and more shining than the thorax. Body beneath black, moderately densely punctured. Legs piceous or black, the tibiæ especially the anterior often paler. Anterior tibiæ finely denticulate; middle and posterior similar, finely spinulose. Length .08—.10 inch; 2—2.5 mm.

The prosternum is narrow, the tip subacutely rounded. Front nearly truncate. Claws simple.

This species and the next are extremely close and it may be a matter of doubt as to whether they should be retained as distinct. They seem to differ in the thoracic margin; here the margin is of equal width from apex to base and is quite distinctly deplanate even to the hind angles. The sides of the thorax seem also arcuate in front of the hind angles so that the base is a little narrowed. Finally the surface here is not alutaceous between the punctures. The color of the antennæ and legs has no value.

Mr. Reitter has sent me a specimen under the name *californicus*, which he considers a variety of the European *M. æneus* Fab., perfectly identical with the present species, and while I presume the determination to be correct our name is retained until further comparisons are made.

Occurs in California and Oregon.

M. mutatus Harold, (*ruficornis* ‖ Lec.)—This species resembles the preceding so closely that merely the slight differences will be detailed: Form slightly more robust, surface subopaque, the interspaces between the punctures distinctly alutaceous. Thoracic margin distinctly deplanate but not of equal width and not attaining the hind angles. At about the posterior fourth of the margin the latter becomes broader, forming a vague depression behind which the margin is not distinctly deplanate. This depression or fovea varies in distinctness, but is never absent as in the preceding species. Length .08—.10 inch; 2—2.5 mm.

The specimens from Kansas and Colorado have usually entirely pale antennæ, although this is by no means constant, a piceous club is often seen on a paler stem. The punctuation of the surface is usually that described in the preceding species, but this is slightly variable also. Specimens from Michigan and New York, are less densely punctured and more shining but still showing more or less of the alutaceous surface. I have tried, but fruitlessly, to separate these forms specifically, but the differences between this and *rufimanus* are already so feeble as to prevent me from going any farther in this direction.

Occurs from New York to Colorado.

M. seminulum Lec.—Oval, slightly oblong, black, shining, sparsely pubescent. Head moderately densely punctured. Thorax twice as wide as long, narrower in front, sides posteriorly feebly, in front more broadly arcuate, hind angles obtusely rectangular, margin very narrow not deplanate, surface not densely punctured. Elytra one-fourth longer than wide, slightly narrowed to apex, surface rather sparsely punctured, shining. Body beneath moderately densely punctured. Anterior tibiæ finely denticulate, middle and posterior finely spinulose. Length .07 inch; 2 mm. nearly.

The epistoma is nearly squarely truncate as in *rufimanus* and the tarsal claws simple. It is known from all our species with simple claws and denticulate tibiæ by the very narrow thoracic margin.

With this species I unite that bearing the name *obsoletus* in Dr. Leconte's cabinet. It appears less shining than the other but this may result from the better preservation of the pubescence. The two are represented by unique specimens.

Oregon and North shore of Lake Superior.

M. pinguis n. sp.—Broadly oval, robust, piceous, feebly shining, sparsely pubescent, surface moderately densely punctate, the elytra more densely than the thorax. The latter nearly twice as wide as long, narrower in front, sides arcuate, more broadly anteriorly, hind angles obtuse, margin narrow not deplanate, disc convex. Elytra as broad as long, convex. Body beneath coarsely punctate, piceous, legs paler. Anterior tibiæ coarsely serrate, middle and posterior tibiæ finely denticulate. Tarsal claws distinctly toothed at base. Prosternum slightly broader behind the coxæ, rounded at tip. Epistoma rather deeply emarginate, the lateral angles acute. Length .10 inch; 2.5 mm.

This species has so many peculiarities that any comparison with the other species is entirely unnecessary. Its broad form is very striking at first sight, the length and breadth are to each other as 10 to 7.

One specimen from the Southern coast of Newfoundland, given to Dr. Lecoute by Mr. L. Reiche of Paris, belonging to Mr. Reitter's subgenus *Acanthogethes* and apparently most closely allied to *M. brevis* St., of Europe.

CYCHRAMINI.

Maxillæ with one lobe. Labrum distinct. Thorax margined at base covering the base of the elytra. Elytra covering the abdomen in great part, the pygidium is part only exposed. Prosternum more or less prolonged at apex. Tarsi distinctly five-jointed.

The genera here placed contain species of broadly oval convex form, either pubescent or glabrous. The tribe as constituted here is the same as that of Erichson and Lacordaire, excepting that *Cybocephalus* has been removed in accordance with the views of Duval, (Gen. Col. Eur.), and *Psilopyga* added.

The genera are distinguished in the following manner:

Mesosternum protuberant in front, the middle coxæ widely separated.
   Prosternum prolonged, dilated laminiform at tip, covering entirely the mesosternum. Body glabrous, elytra striato-punctate...............**Psilopyga.**
   Prosternum less prolonged, feebly dilated at tip, not covering entirely the mesosternum. Body pubescent, elytra irregularly punctate.
                                             Amphicrossus.
Mesosternum small, oblique, not protuberant.
   Metasternum protuberant, widely separating the middle coxæ. Prosternum not prolonged at tip, not laminiform, vertical behind the anterior coxæ. Body glabrous.................................... ....**Cyllodes.**
   Metasternum not protuberant, middle coxæ narrowly separated.
      Hind tarsi longer than the others. Body glabrous.................**Pallodes.**
      Tarsi equal in length. Body pubescent..................... ....**Cychramus.**

PSILOPYGA Lec.

Labrum prominent, deeply bilobed. Front prolonged at middle truncate. Antennæ with an oval, abrupt, three-jointed club, grooves deep subocular, parallel. Mentum transverse, sides short, apex arcuate. Last joint of maxillary palpi cylindrical, rounded at tip, the labial oval. Prosternum prolonged behind the coxæ, the tip broader and explanate covering the mesosternum which is carinate. Thorax margined at base, covering the base of the elytra, the middle with a short but broad, squarely truncate lobe. Scutellum large, broadly triangular. Elytra truncate. Tibiæ with outer apical angle dentiform; anterior tarsi dilated, the middle feebly, the posterior simple. Tarsal claws simple.

The males have a small additional segment.

I have removed this genus from the preceding tribe and place it here from the margined base of the thorax. It seems to me more closely allied to *Pallodes* than any other in our fauna, the large scutellum and the form of the basal margin of the thorax indicating this alliance very plainly.

P. histrina Lec.—Broadly oval, robust, black, shining, glabrous. Head coarsely punctured. Thorax more than twice as wide as long, narrowed in front, apex emarginate, base arcuate with a short broad lobe at middle and slightly sinuate each side, sides regularly arcuate following the curve of the elytra, margin narrow, disc convex not densely punctured, punctures of moderate size with a group of larger punctures forming an arcuate series near the apex. Scutellum moderately densely punctured. Elytra as broad as long, sides regularly arcuate, apex rotundate-truncate, surface with ten rows of moderately coarse punctures, intervals slightly convex, irregularly sparsely punctulate. Body beneath sparsely coarsely punctate. Length .20 inch; 5 mm. (Pl. III, fig. 14).

The resemblance of this insect to a *Histeride* is so complete that it is always placed among them by inexperienced observers.

The anterior tibiæ are simple except the apical prolongation, but when viewed by transmitted light they appear to be finely crenulate. The tarsi are more dilated in the male than in the female, but in both sexes the posterior tarsi are slender.

Occurs in Pennsylvania, Georgia and Missouri, but rare.

P. nigripennis Lec.—Bright rufous, elytra above black. Agrees with the preceding in form and sculpture except as follows : Thorax more sparsely and less coarsely punctured, punctures similar without the arcuate group of coarser punctures. Striæ of elytra less deep, punctures smaller, intervals scarcely convex. Body beneath more sparsely punctate. Length .18 inch; 4.5 mm.

The outer apical angles of the tibiæ are prolonged into longer processes than in *histrina*. (Pl. III, fig. 14, a, b, c.)

I feel very uncertain regarding the status of this species, as I believe that more specimens will show that it is merely a variety of *histrina*, yet as the subject now presents itself they certainly cannot be united.

One specimen, Pennsylvania.

AMPHICROSSUS Erichs.

Labrum bilobed. Mandibles bidentate at tip. Antennal grooves slightly convergent, subocular. Prosternum prolonged at tip, slightly laminiform, anteriorly more or less carinate. Mesosternum prominent. Tibiæ simple. Anterior tarsi distinctly dilated, middle feebly, the posterior nearly simple. Claws not toothed.

The males have an additional segment, visible only beneath, and on the elytra near the middle of the suture a small brush of stiff erect hairs resembling a spine.

Two species occur in our fauna.

Piceous, more or less maculate. Prosternum obtusely carinate. Males with
brush of hairs on elytra...**ciliatus.**
Black. Prosternum acutely carinate. Males without brush of hairs on the
elytra...**niger.**

A. ciliatus Erichs.—Broadly oval, piceous, subopaque, pubescent, elytra
maculate, legs yellowish. Head closely punctate. Thorax more than twice
as wide as long, narrowed in front, apex deeply emarginate, base truncate,
sides feebly arcuate, hind angles broadly rounded, surface moderately closely
punctate, margins paler, fimbriate, disc with pale spot in front of scutellum.
Elytra as long as wide a little narrowed to apex, surface more finely punctured
than the thorax and less densely, color piceous with three pale spots on each
at base, sometimes a fourth near the apex. Body beneath piceous, opaque,
sparsely punctate. Prosternum obtusely carinate. Legs yellowish. Length
.14—.22 inch; 3.5—4.5 mm.

Occurs in Missouri, Georgia and Florida.

A. niger n. sp.—Oval, black above, ferruginous beneath, sparsely pubescent, feebly shining. Prosternum acutely carinate. Males without elytral
brush of hairs. Length .18 inch; 4.5 mm.

The above characters separate this species from the preceding.
The form is less broad, the surface more shining, rather less punctured and pubescent. Above the species is uniformly black, never
maculate.

Occurs in Arizona, under the loose outer bark of the Mesquit.

CYLLODES Erichs.

Labrum short, emarginate. Mandibles simple. Mentum broad,
bisinuate in front, more prominent at middle. Terminal joint of both
palpi cylindrical not dilated. Antennæ with three-jointed, abrupt
club, the grooves short, convergent. Prosternum behind the coxæ
vertical not prolonged at tip, not laminiform. Mesosternum carinate,
usually concealed by the meeting of the pro- and metasternum, the
latter prominent in front. Thorax with a short lobe at middle of
base. Scutellum large, broader than long. Elytra rotundato-truncate,
pygidium partly exposed. Anterior tarsi moderately, middle feebly
dilated, posterior simple. Claws simple. Outer apical angle of tibiæ
acute but not spiniform.

The males have an extremely small additional segment, which
might easily escape observation.

C. biplagiatus Lec.—Broadly oval, black, shining, glabrous, each elytron
with an oval red spot near the base. Head and thorax moderately closely
punctate. Thorax more than twice as wide as long, narrowed in front, apex
emarginate, base arcuate with a short broad, scutellar lobe, sides moderately

arcuate, hind angles rectangular. Scutellum large, moderately densely punctate. Elytra as wide as long, disc with seven rows of moderately coarse punctures, the intervals irregularly punctate. Body beneath sparsely punctate. Legs black, tarsi paler. Length .16—.18 inch; 4—4.5 mm.

This insect at first sight resembles a *Hyperaspis*. The elytra should have ten rows of punctures, but the first and the outer two are entirely obsolete and replaced by the confused punctures.

Occurs in Massachusetts.

PALLODES Erichs.

Mandibles bifid at tip. Prosternum slightly prolonged not dilated at tip. Mesosternum not carinate, middle coxæ not widely separated. Anterior and middle tarsi dilated, posterior slender as long as the tibiæ. Outer apical angle of tibiæ obtusely rounded.

The males have an extremely short additional segment.

The characters other than those given above are the same as in the preceding genus.

One species is known to me.

P. silaceus Erichs.—Oval, convex, pale piceo-testaceous, glabrous, shining, elytra iridescent. Head sparsely punctate. Thorax very sparsely and finely punctate, more than twice as wide as long, much narrowed in front, apex emarginate, base feebly arcuate, at middle a very short, truncate scutellar lobe, sides arcuate, hind angles rectangular. Scutellum large, sparsely punctate. Elytra longer than wide, narrower toward apex, slightly broader behind the humeri, disc with nine rows of moderate punctures the sutural deeply impressed, intervals with a single series of very fine punctures. Body beneath smooth. Length .12—.16 inch; 3—4 mm.

The elytra are sometimes darker externally near the tip. The tibial spurs on the anterior two pairs of feet are very small, those on the posterior very long.

Occurs in the Middle and Southern Atlantic region.

CYCHRAMUS Kug.

Labrum feebly emarginate. Mandibles simple at tip. Antennal grooves short, convergent. Prosternum vertical behind the coxæ the tip not prolonged. Mesosternum vertical, not carinate, the middle coxæ not very widely separated. Thorax not lobed at middle of base. Scutellum not large. Tarsi all dilated.

The males have a small additional segment.

This genus is allied to *Amphicrossus* in form and pubescent surface, but differs in the bilobed labrum, the form of mesosternum and the tarsi. In the present genus the mesosternum is narrow and oblique, the metasternum flexed upwards at tip between the coxæ and not protuberant.

Two species occur in our fauna.

Tibiæ not prolonged at tip, the middle not sinuate externally.........**adustus.**
Tibiæ especially the anterior with the outer apical angle prolonged, the middle
moderately deeply sinuate before the apex..................**Zimmermanni.**

C. adustus Erichs.—Broadly oval, convex, opaque, pubescent, ferruginous
elytra variable from entirely ferruginous to entirely black. Head sparsely
punctured, front sinuously transversely impressed. Thorax twice as wide as
long, narrower in front, apex deeply emarginate, base truncate, hind angles
obtusely rectangular or rounded, sides arcuate, margin narrow with fine fimbriæ,
surface rather coarsely and closely punctate. Elytra as broad as long, slightly
narrower posteriorly, margin finely fimbriate, apex obtusely truncate, disc with
fine elongate punctures arranged in quite regular series. Body beneath sparsely
punctate. Length .12—.16 inch; 3—4 mm. (Pl. III, fig. 18, d, e, f.)

The tibiæ are all gradually broader to apex, the outer apical angle
not prolonged. The variation in color of the elytra is from ferruginous to black by the sides becoming piceous, this color extends so
that merely a sutural triangle is ferruginous, finally the entire color of
the elytra is black, forming the variety *bicolor* of the Check List.

Occurs in Virginia, Georgia and Missouri, not common.

C. Zimmermanni n. sp.—Oval, convex, subopaque, pubescent, elytra
piceous. Head sparsely granular, front transversely impressed. Thorax twice
as wide as long, narrower in front, apex deeply emarginate, base truncate, sides
arcuate, hind angles obtusely rounded, surface moderately closely punctured,
punctures submuricate, margin finely fimbriate. Elytra as wide as long, arcuately narrowed to tip, convex, disc faintly substriate, intervals finely submuri-
cately punctured. Body beneath moderately closely punctate, the prosternum
smooth. Length .18 inch; 4.5 mm. (Pl. III, fig. 18, a, b, c.)

Anterior tibiæ feebly sinuate on the outer side the apical angle prolonged into a long acute tooth, middle tibiæ sinuate externally the apical
angle moderately prolonged, posterior tibiæ feebly sinuate the apical
angle more prolonged than the middle but much less than in the anterior.

This species of which I have seen but one specimen resembles the
variety *bicolor* of the preceding species. It is a little less broad and
differs in sculpture also. The variation in the form of the tibiæ does
not seem to me to be of generic value, as similar characters are already
foreshadowed in *Meligethes* and *Psilopyga.*

One specimen, South Carolina, collected by the late Dr. Chas.
Zimmermann.

CYBOCEPHALINI.

Maxillæ with one lobe. Tarsi four-jointed. Body retractile, mandibles in repose resting against the metasternum. Thorax margined at
base, covering the base of the elytra.

The views of Duval in separating this genus from the *Cychramini,*
seem to me correct and worthy of adoption.

CYBOCEPHALUS Erichs.

Labrum entire. Mandibles acute at tip, a small tooth posteriorly. Epistoma slightly prolonged at middle. Antennæ scarcely longer than the width of the head, the antennal grooves small and convergent. Prosternum acutely carinate in front, not prolonged behind the anterior coxæ which are very narrowly closed behind. Mesosternum broad, oblique, metasternum slightly protuberant. Thorax margined at base, sides very short. Scutellum rather large. Tibiæ simple, tarsi slightly dilated, four-jointed, claws simple.

The males have a rather large additional segment.

The head is broad and deflexed, the mandibles resting against the metasternum. The body is, in contraction, ovate and very convex.

After a careful examination of the tarsi I am convinced that Duval is correct and that there are but four joints, and that the claws are simple.

The resemblance of the species of this genus to *Liodes* is so very great, that it might be considered quite pardonable to confuse them without a careful examination of the anterior coxæ and antennæ. The front of *Liodes* is truncate or broadly rounded, in *Cybocephalus* prolonged at middle.

Two species occur in our fauna.

Surface black shining, thoracic margin with extremely narrow translucent border, not at all explanate..**nigritulus.**
Surface with distinct æneous lustre, thoracic margin translucent and distinctly explanate...**californicus.**

C. nigritulus Lec.—Ovate, contractile, convex, black, very shining. Legs piceous. Head and thorax smooth, but under very high power very finely alutaceous, sides of thorax with extreme margin narrowly translucent not explanate. Elytra with extremely minute punctures very sparsely placed in the basal region, sides and apex absolutely smooth but under high power finely alutaceous. Body beneath coarsely punctate. Length .04 inch; 1 mm. (Pl. III, fig. 15.)

When the specimens are stretched out they are about one-half nearly longer.

Occurs in Michigan and Georgia.

C. californicus n. sp.—Black, surface æneous and under high power distinctly alutaceous. Thorax with lateral margin slightly explanate and translucent. Elytra under moderate power distinctly but very sparsely punctulate, smooth at sides and base. Length .03 inch; .75 mm.

The length extended is about one-half greater. From the preceding species this is known by the sides of thorax quite distinctly explanate and more broadly translucent than in *nigritulus*. The punctuation of the elytra is also more evident and the surface quite distinctly æneous.

San Diego and Calaveras (Crotch), Owens' Valley, California.

Cybocephalus? unicolor Motsch., Bull. Mosc. 1845, iv, p. 364, does not belong to the genus.

IPINI.

Maxillæ with one lobe. Labrum connate with the front, suture more or less distinct. Antennæ eleven-jointed, terminated by a three-jointed club. Anterior coxæ open behind, narrowly enclosed in *Pityophagus*.

By the one character this tribe is distinguished from all the Nitidulidæ. By all authors from Erichson, the labrum is said to be concealed by the front, that this is not the true condition is very easily seen and proved by dissection.

The genera composing the tribe are as follows:

Anterior coxæ open behind.
    Thorax margined at base, slightly overlapping the base of the elytra. Body pubescent....................**Cryptarcha.**
    Thorax not margined at base. Body glabrous....................**Ips.**
Anterior coxæ closed behind.
    Thorax not margined at base. Body glabrous....................**Pityophagus.**

In the above arrangement *Cryptarcha* leads naturally to the *Cychramini*, and *Pityophagus* to the Rhizophagidæ. *Cryptarcha* is restricted to the Atlantic region, the other two genera have representatives on both sides of the continent.

CRYPTARCHA Shuck.

Labrum indistinct. Mandibles feebly bifid at tip. Antennal grooves short, convergent. Prosternum prolonged and laminiform at tip, partly concealing the mesosternum, anterior coxæ open behind. Thorax margined at base. Scutellum not large. Tibiæ simple, tarsi dilated, claws simple. (Pl. III, fig. 12, *a, b, c*.)

The males have the tips of the elytra obliquely sinuate as in some *Ips*, there is no additional segment. The head is larger in the male than in the female.

Three species occur in our fauna.

Elytra substriately punctured, surface simply pubescent.
    Sides of thorax not explanate, of elytra very narrowly reflexed......**ampla.**
Elytra irregularly, moderately densely punctured, surface pubescent and with rows of short erect setæ.
    Sides of thorax not explanate, of elytra very narrowly reflexed...**strigata.**
    Sides of thorax explanate, of elytra rather widely reflexed.......**concinna.**

C. ampla Erichs.—Oval, more obtuse in front, piceous, sparsely pubescent. Thorax feebly emarginate in front, sides feebly arcuate and but little narrowed anteriorly, margin narrowly reflexed but not explanate, hind angles obtuse, surface moderately closely punctate. Elytra gradually narrowing posteriorly, margin feebly reflexed, apices separately rounded, more oblique in the male, surface substriately punctate, sparsely pubescent, without erect setæ. Length .24—.28 inch; 6—7 mm.

The male has the head larger than the female and the thorax broader in front, the elytral apex oblique.

This species differs from the next two by its much larger size, uniformly piceous color.

Occurs in the Middle, Southern and Western States, not rare.

C. strigata Fab.—Oval, broader in front, piceous, moderately shining, sparsely pubescent, and with short erect setæ. Thorax nearly twice as wide as long, sides gradually arcuate and narrowed to the front, hind angles rectangular, margin not explanate, narrowly reflexed, color piceous, margin paler, surface not densely punctate, sparsely pubescent and with a few erect setæ. Elytra very little longer than wide, sides feebly arcuate and gradually narrowed to apex, margin very narrowly reflexed, color piceous and with two transverse sinuous fasciæ more or less interrupted and a scutellar spot pale testaceous, surface sparsely pubescent and with seven series of short erect setæ the outer rather irregular. Body beneath piceous, sparsely punctulate. Length .10—.14 inch; 2.5—3.5 mm.

Occurs in Europe and our Atlantic States.

C. concinna Mels.—This species is more regularly oval, less narrowed posteriorly; the color is similar to *strigata*, differs also in having the sides of the thorax moderately explanate and the elytral margin wider and more reflexed. The sinuous fasciæ of the elytra are usually entire, sometimes interrupted by the suture. Length .08—.12 inch; 2—3 mm.

In both these species the elytra are obliquely prolonged in the male, obtuse in the female.

With this species I unite *C. bella* Reitter, which does not differ from the Melsheimer species, *concinna* ‡ Reitter, seems to be a mere color variety of *strigata*.

Middle States, Kansas, Texas.

IPS Fab.

Labrum connate with the epistoma, suture more or less evident. Front slightly prolonged. Mandibles stout, bifid at tip. Prosternum prolonged at tip, never attaining the metasternum, anterior coxæ open behind. Antennæ with an abrupt club, grooves moderately deep, convergent. Tarsi dilated or not, claws simple.

There is an additional segment in the male, but often so much retracted as to be invisible.

Here is a proper occasion to call attention to the labrum. All authors speak of that organ as *concealed* by the epistoma. This is not the case, the labrum is not concealed but is very evident beyond the epistoma and is connate therewith, the suture quite evident in all the species, more especially in *obtusus*. (Pl. III, fig. 23).

The following tables give the arrangement of the species:

Hind tarsi nearly as broadly dilated as the anterior; thorax broader at base than apex...Sub-Genus **IPS.**
Hind tarsi slender; thorax narrower at base.....Sub-Genus **GLISCHROCHILUS.**

Sub-Genus IPS.

Middle and hind tibiæ ♂ suddenly broader at apical half.
  Black, each elytron with two large red spots............................**obtusus.**
Middle and hind tibiæ not different in the sexes.
  Body beneath black...**fasciatus.**
  Metasternum and abdomen red...........................**sanguinolentus.**

Sub-Genus GLISCHROCHILUS.

Sides of thorax distinctly sinuate posteriorly.
  Elytra coarsely punctured, with large discal reddish space enclosing black spots...**confluentus.**
  Elytra more finely punctured, black, with short, linear testaceous lines.
                                           vittatus.
Sides of thorax gradually convergent posteriorly, straight not sinuate.
  Elytra black, with a subhumeral red spot and a median interrupted fascia.
                                    cylindricus.

I. obtusus Say.—Piceous black, elytra each with two red spots, one at the middle of base, the other slightly behind the middle. Length .36—.48 inch; 9—12 mm.

The males have the middle and posterior tibiæ suddenly broader at apical half. A small additional segment is also visible, the pygidium truncate at tip and not concave. (Pl. III, fig. 23, *a*, *b*.)

The females have simple tibiæ, pygidium oval at apex and slightly concave near the end.

In both sexes the elytra agree in the form of the apices of the elytra, they are very slightly oblique in both sexes.

Occurs in the Middle and Southern Atlantic States.

I. fasciatus Oliv.—Black, shining, elytra normally with a broad basal and a subapical fascia yellow. Length .16—.28 inch; 4—7 mm.

The males have the small additional segment and the tips of the elytra oblique, slightly prolonged.

The females have rounded elytral tips. The tibiæ are not different in the two sexes.

The markings on the elytra vary from the fasciate form by the gradual decrease of the size of the spots, so that there finally remain two punctiform spots on each elytron, one basal, the other post-median.

Occurs everywhere in the eastern United States, extending to Oregon and Vancouver.

I. sanguinolentus Oliv.—Piceous black, abdomen red, elytra in great part red, the tip, small humeral and larger discal spot black. Length .18—.24 inch; 4.5—6 mm.

The sexual characters are precisely as in *fasciatus*.

The elytra vary in color by the extension of the discal black spot so that very little red remains, this is the variety *subromaculatus* Reitter.

Occurs from Canada to Florida and Texas.

I. confluentus Say.—Piceous, elongate, coarsely punctured, sides of thorax sinuate posteriorly. Elytra reddish testaceous, tip black, an oblique humeral band, broader at tip, suture at base narrowly piceous, a small spot on each side of scutellum piceous. Length .18—.20 inch; 4.5—5 mm.

Sexual characters as in *fasciatus*.

The markings of this species seem to be merely a modification of that of *sanguinolentus*, in which the discal spot extends obliquely to the humeri and the small spot on each side of scutellum is added.

Occurs from Canada to Georgia.

I. vittatus Say.—Resembles the preceding in form, but more finely punctured and less convex. Elytra with short linear testaceous spots. Length .16—.20 inch; 4—5 mm.

Sexual characters as in *fasciatus*, but with the apices of the elytra ♂ a little more prolonged.

This species has been thought to be a variety of the preceding, but it is more elongate and depressed and with finer punctuation.

Occurs in Canada, Colorado, Utah, and extends to California, Oregon and Alaska.

I. cylindricus Lec.—Elongate, moderately convex, piceous, sparsely punctate, elytra with subhumeral spot and post-median interrupted fascia red. Sides of thorax convergent posteriorly, straight. Length .26—.30 inch; 6.5—7.5 mm.

Sexual characters as in *fasciatus*.

Occurs in California, Oregon and Nevada.

PITYOPHAGUS Shuck.

Labrum connate with the front, suture feebly distinct. Mandibles bifid at tip. Front slightly prolonged. Prosternum not prolonged at tip, anterior coxæ closed behind. Antennæ with an abrupt three-jointed club, grooves convergent. Tarsi dilated, claws simple. Tibiæ finely spinous externally. (Pl. III, fig. 27).

The males have an additional segment scarcely more visible than in *Ips*. The elytra are squarely truncate in both sexes.

The species known to me are as follows :

Head convex without vertical fovea or occipital groove..............**cephalotes.**
Head convex with fine longitudinal occipital groove..............**rufipennis.**
Head convex with deep vertical fovea................................**verticalis.**

P. cephalotes is piceous with a paler thorax, *rufipennis* has paler elytra, *verticalis* is more depressed than either and uniformly piceous, the first is from the eastern region, the second from the Pacific coast, the third from Colorado.

P. cephalotes Lec.—Elongate, subcylindrical, rufo-piceous, elytra darker. Head convex without impressions, rather coarsely but sparsely punctured. Thorax scarcely wider than the head, a little longer than wide, sides straight, base feebly arcuate, coarsely but sparsely punctured, a vague smooth median line, punctures somewhat elongate. Elytra very little wider than the thorax, humeral angles dentiform, coarsely and moderately densely punctured, punctures finer at sides and tip. Body beneath sparsely punctate. Length .20 inch; 5 mm.

One ♀ specimen, Pennsylvania.

P. rufipennis Horn.—Piceous black, elytra brownish red. Head with a fine longitudinal occipital groove. Thorax sparsely punctured, punctures not elongate, sides very slightly arcuate posteriorly. Elytra less coarsely punctured than the preceding. Length .24—.28 inch; 6—7 mm.

Quite distinct from the preceding species, but equally convex and otherwise colored and sculptured.

Occurs in Oregon and Vancouver.

P. verticalis n. sp.—Elongate, depressed, subcylindrical, piceous, legs paler. Head coarsely and moderately densely punctured, a deep vertical fovea. Thorax not longer than wide, narrowed posteriorly, sides nearly straight, feebly arcuate posteriorly, surface with elongate punctures sparsely placed. Elytra not densely punctured, punctures coarser near the base and slightly elongate. Body beneath sparsely punctate. Length .26 inch; 6.5 mm.

The tibiæ of the specimen before me are devoid of the usual small spinules, but this is probably owing to abrasion.

One ♂ Colorado, (Morrison).

SMICRIPINI.

Labrum moderately prominent. Maxillæ one lobed. Mentum transverse concealing the maxillæ. Antennæ eleven-jointed with a three-jointed club. Tarsi three jointed. Anterior coxæ open behind.

With these words an aberrant tribe is characterized which exhibits affinities with the great central mass of Nitidulidæ, and in another direction less strongly with the Monotomidæ. A discussion of the question occurs farther on.

There is but one genus at present known.

SMICRIPS Lec.

Labrum moderately prominent, transverse, truncate. Frontal suture arcuate, deeply impressed. Mentum transverse, twice as wide as long, slightly narrowed in front, apex emarginate, at middle slightly depressed. Ligula prominent, palpi short, last joint not dilated. Maxillæ entirely concealed by the mentum, with one lobe only which is fimbriate at tip and along the inner margin; palpi not longer than the lobe, the first joint slender, second and third suddenly stouter, fourth conical, as long as the two preceding united. Mandibles broadly triangular, slightly bifid at tip, slightly sinuate on the inner border, at base clasping the sides of the mentum. Eyes round, moderately prominent. Head not constricted behind. Antennæ free at base, eleven-jointed, first joint stout. cylindrical, second similar but shorter, 3—8 small, nearly equal, 9—11 rather suddenly broader, forming an elongate club; grooves subocular, short, feeble, slightly convergent. Anterior coxæ transverse, trochantin distinct, the cavities open behind, tip of prosternum not elevated nor prolonged. Mesosternum horizontal. Middle coxæ moderately distant, obliquely oval, their cavities open externally, closed by the mesosternal epimera. Posterior coxæ oval widely separated, the intercoxal process arcuate at tip. Abdomen with five segments, first and fifth equal in length and equal to the three intermediate segments united, these latter are short and equal. Tibiæ slender, spurs minute. Tarsi moderately dilated three-jointed, first two joints short. equal, last joint more than twice as long as the other two united. Claws arcuate, simple. Elytra truncate, pygidium exposed.

The male has a very distinct additional segment.

It is not without diffidence that I claim for this insect a place among the Nitidulidæ, and in order that this position may be made more evident I have given the very extended generic description above. The parts of the mouth have been described from actual dissections, a matter of no small difficulty in an insect so minute, but thanks to the kind practical instruction of the Rev. A. Matthews of England, whose dissections of Trichopterygidæ are still the wonder of the scientific world, I have been enabled to overcome the difficulties involved.

I cannot see that this insect has any claim to be considered a Monotomide, beyond the three-jointed tarsi and the impression of the frontal suture which is not however characteristic of that family. The characters which especially forbid its entrance there are—transverse anterior and middle coxæ, maxillæ with a single lobe, antennæ

eleven-jointed with a three-jointed, not compact club. The relative
length of the abdominal segments is that of the Monotomidæ, but
a similar structure is very closely approximated in Nitidulidæ. The
anterior coxæ are here open behind but widely closed in all known
Monotomidæ, although this character varies in the Nitidulidæ. In
view of the divergences and affinities above shown the weight seems
to me more in favor of the Nitidulidæ than the Monotomidæ.
One species only is known.

S. palmicola Lec.—Elongate, rufo-testaceous, sparsely pubescent, minutely
punctulate above and beneath but more evidently on the thorax. Thorax a
little wider than long, slightly narrowed in front, apex truncate, base feebly
arcuate, sides straight. Elytra a little wider than the thorax, a little longer
than the head and thorax together, sides very feebly arcuate, apices truncate.
Pygidium moderately coarsely punctate. Length .04 inch; 1 mm.; varying a
little more and less. (Pl. III, fig. 1, with details.)

The elytra have often a darker cloud at tip and base.

The last ventral segment ♂ is truncate, and the additional dorsal
segment visible.

Occurs in Florida, on the Palmetto.

RHIZOPHAGINI.

Labrum visible at the tip of the epistoma but connate with it.
Mandibles simple at tip. Maxillæ with two lobes, the outer slender
not capitate. Antennæ ten-jointed, club of two joints, the tenth partly
enclosed; antennal grooves short, convergent. Prosternum not prolonged at tip. Anterior coxal cavities closed behind. Mesosternum
horizontal. Intercoxal process triangular, acute. Abdomen with the
first and fifth segments long, the intermediate three short, equal.
Elytra truncate, pygidium exposed. Tarsi feebly dilated, heteromerous
in the males, pentamerous in the females. Claws simple.

The males in addition to the tarsal character have an additional
segment and the head usually larger.

The ten-jointed antennæ distinguish this tribe from the others.
In the aggregate of their organization there is an approach toward
the Trogositidæ from which the structure of the tarsi alone distinguishes them. In the present tribe the first tarsal joint is as long
or a little longer than the second, while in the Trogositidæ the first
joint is small. By its bilobed maxillæ *Rhizophagus* approaches the
Brachypterini on the one hand and Trogositidæ on the other; the
large additional segment of the male and the structure of the abdomen
with the first and last joints short are Carpophilide, while the form of
the head and connate labrum are Ipide. The tribe seems therefore

to be osculant with Trogositide tendencies, in the same way that Smicripini have feeble Monotomide affinities.

Mr. Reitter has described a genus IXION, in which the tarsi are said to be 4—4—3 in the male.

One genus only is known in our fauna. The species are as follows:

Thorax longer than wide..1.
Thorax as wide or wider than long...4.
1.—Elytra with distinctly impressed striæ which attain the tip and punctured
    their entire length...**sculpturatus** Mann.
    Elytra with rows of punctures merely...2.
2.—Thorax in ♂ very decidedly narrowed from apex to base, sides nearly
    straight; thorax beneath nearly smooth.............**cylindricus** Lec.
    Thorax in ♂ scarcely or not narrowed posteriorly, sides in both sexes
    feebly arcuate; thorax beneath punctured...3.
3.—Elytra wider than thorax; color piceous, rufous at base.
                                                dimidiatus Mann.
    Elytra wider than thorax; color uniformly brown.......**brunneus** Horn.
    Elytra not wider; color pitchy black, each with two rufous spots.
                                                bipunctatus (Say).
4.—Prosternum and side pieces coarsely and moderately densely punctured;
    epipleuræ distinctly punctured at base............**approximatus** Lec.
    Prosternum and side pieces sparsely punctured; epipleuræ smooth.
    Elytra pitchy black..**remotus** Lec.
    Elytra each with two oblique rufous spots on each......**minutus** Mann.

R. sculpturatus Mann.—Piceous or rufo-piceous, moderately depressed. Head moderately but not densely punctate, front with a feeble impression on each side. Third joint of antennæ slightly longer than the two following. Thorax longer than wide, sides feebly arcuate and gradually narrowed to base; disc at middle subdepressed, surface coarsely but not densely punctured at middle, finely punctured at the sides. Elytra not wider than the apex of the thorax, disc subdepressed, sides feebly arcuate at apical half; surface distinctly striate, striæ entire but feebler at apex and with moderately coarse punctures closely placed but not serrate, intervals flat. Prosternum very sparsely punctured at middle, sides and side pieces coarsely and densely punctured. Metasternum and abdomen coarsely but sparsely punctured. Pygidium coarsely punctured. Length .14 inch; 3.5 mm.

The color of this species is variable, four specimens in my cabinet are decidedly ferruginous, others are piceous, while one exhibits distinct evidences of having the elytra piceous with a humeral and subapical paler spot. One specimen in my cabinet from New York, differs in having the elytra still more deeply striate. I am unwilling to separate it as distinct on the one specimen.

Occurs in Vancouver, Nevada and New York.

R. cylindricus Lec.—Elongate, cylindrical, rufo-piceous. Head sparsely and finely punctured, more coarsely at sides and occiput. Third joint of antennæ nearly as long as the three following united. Thorax longer than wide, sides straight and gradually convergent ♂ or very feebly arcuate ♀;

disc convex, sparsely and finely punctured. Elytra cylindrical, parallel, convex, sutural striæ impressed at apical half, surface with rows of moderate punctures which become obsolete near the tip. Prothorax beneath smooth, metathorax and abdomen sparsely and finely punctured, last ventral more evidently punctured. Pygidium sparsely punctate. Length .18 inch; 4.5 mm.

This is the largest species in our fauna. In the male the head is larger than in the female and rather broader than the thorax, in both the front is convex without impressions and the mandibles of the male are rather more prominent than the female.

Occurs in Tenuessee and Georgia.

R. dimidiatus Mann.—Elongate, subcylindrical, piceous, base of elytra, head and legs rufous. Head sparsely punctulate, front slightly impressed on each side. Antennæ with third joint hardly equal to the next two united. Thorax longer than wide, rather sparsely and finely punctate, sides very feebly arcuate in both sexes, narrowed slightly to base in male. Elytra slightly wider than the thorax, subcylindrical, sides at apical half slightly narrowing to apex, sutural striæ at apical half slightly impressed, disc with rows of fine punctures becoming rapidly obsolete to apex. Prosternum at middle sparsely punctured, sides and side pieces coarsely punctured. Abdomen sparsely and equally punctate. Pygidium moderately punctate. Length .14—.16 inch; 3.5—4 mm.

As in the preceding species the male has the head larger than the female but not much so. Its color varies somewhat in the extent of the rufous portion of the elytra but greater or less traces always remain of that color.

Occurs from Alaska to Lake Superior, and Mount Washington, New Hampshire, (Blanchard).

R. brunneus Horn.—Uniformly brownish, moderately shining. Head sparsely punctate. Thorax a little longer than wide, apex and base truncate, sides subparallel at middle, slightly arcuate at base and apex, disc convex, coarsely and sparsely punctured. Elytra slightly wider at base than the thorax and feebly emarginate, disc with rows of moderately coarse punctures which become somewhat finer toward the tip. Prosternum coarsely punctured, side pieces nearly smooth. Metasternum smooth at middle. Abdomen coarsely and sparsely punctured, the first segment smooth at middle. Pygidium sparsely punctate. Length .12 inch; 3 mm.

Marquette, Lake Superior. The punctures of the entire surface are coarser than in any other of our species. It must be considered the intermediate form between those with the long and those with the broad thorax.

R. bipunctatus Say.—Elongate, cylindrical, black shining, antennæ and legs rufous, elytra each with two rufous spots, one oblique behind the base, the other smaller, oval at apical third. Head sparsely punctate. Antennæ with third joint hardly as long as the next two combined. Thorax longer than wide, sides very feebly arcuate, not perceptibly narrowed posteriorly, disc convex sparsely punctulate. Elytra not wider than thorax, cylindrical, parallel, sutural stria impressed at apical half, surface with rows of moderate punctures, rather closely placed, becoming finer at apex but still distinct. Epipleuræ distinctly punctured at base. Prosternum sparsely punctured at middle, densely and more coarsely at the sides, side pieces sparsely punctured. Abdomen coarsely but sparsely punctured. Pygidium coarsely and moderately densely punctured. Length .10—.12 inch; 2.5—3 mm.

The sexes scarcely differ in the form of the head and thorax.

Specimens occur in which the rufous spots of the elytra are not apparent, and varieties may also occur (although I have not seen such), in which the spots spread so as to leave merely the margin and apex piceous.

This species occurs most abundantly in Canada and. the States bordering the great lakes.

R. approximatus Lec.—Piceous, subdepressed, antennæ and legs rufous. Head moderately punctured, rather more coarsely at sides and base, frontal impressions moderate. Third joint of antennæ equal to the next two together. Thorax distinctly wider than long, sides moderately arcuate, hind angles broadly rounded, surface with moderately coarse punctures not densely placed but equally distributed. Elytra subdepressed, not wider than the thorax, sides slightly arcuate at basal half, surface feebly striate, striæ with moderately coarse punctures rather closely placed, becoming somewhat finer toward the apex. Prosternum rather coarsely and moderately densely punctured, side pieces more coarsely punctured. Epipleuræ distinctly punctured at base. Abdomen coarsely punctured. Pygidium moderately densely punctate. Length .12 inch; 3 mm.

I have seen but one ♀ specimen of this species. It closely resembles the next, but is easily known by the sculpture of the under surface and the more closely punctured striæ.

One specimen from New York.

R. remotus Lec.—Piceous, moderately convex, antennæ and legs rufous. Head coarsely but sparsely punctured, more finely in front. Antennæ with third joint as long as the two following. Thorax slightly wider than long, sides feebly arcuate, hind angles broadly rounded, surface moderately and equally punctate. Elytra nearly parallel, moderately convex, surface with striæ of moderately coarse punctures rather closely placed, gradually finer to tip. Thorax beneath sparsely and rather finely punctured. Epipleuræ smooth. Abdomen with first segment rather finely and sparsely punctured, segments two to five more coarsely. Pygidium moderately punctate. Length .10 inch; 2.5 mm.

Occurs in Pennsylvania and Canada.

R. minutus Mann.—Form subdepressed, piceous, shining, legs and antennæ rufous, elytra each with two rufous spots which at times become suffused and cover the entire disc. Head sparsely punctate obsoletely alutaceous. Antennæ with third joint as long as the next two together. Thorax slightly wider than long, sides feebly arcuate and very slightly narrowed posteriorly, disc moderately and evenly punctate, intervals obsoletely alutaceous. Elytra not wider than the thorax, parallel, with rows of moderate punctures which are rather closely placed, becoming finer toward the tip. Epipleuræ smooth at base.

Prosternum very sparsely punctate, side pieces nearly smooth. Abdomen with first segment sparsely punctate, segments two to five more coarsely and densely punctured. Pygidium moderately punctate. Length .10 inch ; 2.5 mm.

The elytra are normally colored as described above, that is, there is an oblique rufous spot on each elytron behind the base and another at apical third. These spots gradually spread so that the entire disc is rufous, and only the side margin and tip piceous. The latter form is that described by Mannerheim.

Specimens have been sent from Oregon, (Ulke), Michigan, (Schwarz, 1599), Canada and Alaska, (Mann.).

The following species is unknown to me. The name is already pre-occupied and it would be as well to drop it entirely from the lists.

Rh. puncticollis ‖ Boh. Res. Eugen. 1858, p. 39.—Elongatus, subdepressus, rufo-ferrugineus, nitidus; prothorace oblongo, sat crebre, evidenter punctulato, lateribus rectis, antice postecceque angustatis ; elytris sat crebre punctato-striatis, interstitus lævibus. Long. 2.75—3 ; lat. .75 mm.
Patria : California, San Francisco.

The detailed description adds nothing of moment to the above short diagnosis. It may not be a Rhizophagus and all of Boheman's localities are uncertain, and as the name is preoccupied it would be better to drop it entirely.

In a short paper in the *Verhandlungen des naturforschenden Vereins in Brünn*, vol. xi, 1872, Mr. Reitter describes as *Rhizophagus* :

R. corpulentus (Motsch.), Reitter = Hesperobænus abbreviatus *Motsch.*

R. striolatus Reitter = Bactridium striolatum.

R. nanus Erichs. = Bactridium ephippigerum *Guér.*

Bibliography and Synonymy.

BRACHYPTERINI.
BRACHYPTERUS Kugelann.
Schneid. Magaz. p. 560.
B. urticæ Fab. Ent. Syst. i, p. 235; Erichs. Nat. Ins. iii, p. 132; Murray, Monogr. Trans. Linn. Soc. xxiv, 3, p. 242.
pusillus Mels. (*Cercus*), Proc. Acad. 1844, p. 105.
B. troglodytes Murr. loc. cit. p. 244.
B. globularius Murr. loc. cit. p. 245.

CERCUS Latreille.
Prec. car. génér. des Ins. p. 68.
C. abdominalis Erichs. Germ. Zeits. 1843, iv, p. 229; Murray, Mon. p. 236.
C. pennatus Murr. Mon. p. 235, ♀.
crinitus Murr. Mon. p. 237, ☿ .

C. sericans Lec. Proc. Acad. 1859, p. 69; Murr. Mon. p. 238.

C. bipustulatus Payk. Fauna Suecc. i, p. 286; Murr. Mon. p. 232.

AMARTUS Lec.
Proc. Acad. 1861, p. 343.

A. tinctus Mann. (*Strongylus?*), Bull. Mosc. 1843, ii, p. 255; Murr. Mon. p. 249,
pl. 32, fig. 8.
ferrugatus Murr. Mon. p. 250.

A. rufipes Lec. Proc. Acad. 1861, p. 344; Murr. Mon. p. 239, pl. 32, fig. 4, c—h.

ANTHONÆUS n. g.
A. agavensis Crotch, (*Colastus*), Trans. Am. Ent. Soc. 1874, p. 76.

CARPOPHILINI.

CARPOPHILUS Stephens.
Illust. of Brit. Entom. iii, p. 50.

C. yucoæ Crotch, (*Colastus*), loc. cit. p. 75.

C. hemipterus Linn. (*Dermestes*), Syst. Nat. i, 2, p. 565; Murr. Mon. p. 362,
pl. 32, fig. 10.
bimaculatus Mels. Proc. Acad. ii, p. 105.

C. pallipennis Say, (*Cercus*), Journ. Acad. iii, p. 194; Murr. Mon. p. 372.
floralis Er. Germ. Zeitschr. iv, p. 261.

C. dimidiatus Fab. (*Nitid.*), Ent. Syst. i, p. 261; Murr. Mon. p. 379.
mutilatus Er. Germ. Zeitschr. iv, p. 258.
luridus Murr. Mon. p. 377.

C. melanopterus Erichs. Germ. Zeitschr. iv, p. 262; Murr. Mon. p. 371, pl. 32,
fig. 11.
rufus Murr. Mon. p. 371.

C. tempestivus Erichs. Germ. Zeitschr. iv, p. 260; Murr. Mon. p. 389.

C. decipiens n. sp.

C. niger Say, (*Cercus*), Journ. Acad. iii, p. 185; Erichs. loc. cit. p. 263; Murr.
Mon. p. 356.
lugubris Murr. Mon. p. 355.

C. marginatus Erichs. Germ. Zeitschr. p. 262; Murr. Mon. p. 390.
minutus Mels. Proc. Acad. ii, p. 105.

C. corticinus Erichs. loc. cit. p. 263; Murr. Mon. p. 351.

C. brachypterus Say, (*Nitid.*), Journ. Acad. v, p. 183; Murr. Mon. p. 388.
humilis Erichs. loc. cit. p. 262.
carbonatus Lec. Col. Kansas, 1859, p. 6.

C. discoideus Lec. Proc. Acad. 1858, p. 62; Murr. Mon. p. 391.
caudalis Lec. (*Tribrachys*), Proc. Acad. 1859, p. 70.

C. antiquus Mels. (*Cercus*), Proc. Acad. 1844, p. 105; Murr. Mon. p. 349.
punctulatus Mels. loc. cit. p. 104.

COLASTUS Erichs.
Germ. Zeitschr. iv, 1843, p. 236.

C. morio Erichs. loc. cit. p. 242; Murr. Mon. p. 270.

C. maculatus Erichs. loc. cit. p. 244.

C. semitectus Say, (*Nitidula*), Journ. Acad. v, p. 182; Erichs. loc. cit. p. 243;
Murr. Mon. p. 277; Lacord. Genera Atl. pl. 18, fig. 1.

C. unicolor Say, (*Nitid.*), loc. cit. p. 183; Murr. Mon. p. 281.
obscurus Erichs. loc. cit. p. 244.

C. truncatus Randall, (*Nitid.*), Bost. Journ. ii, p. 18; Erichs. loc. cit. p. 245 ;
    Murr. Mon. p. 281.
    limbatus Lec. Proc. Acad. 1858, p. 62 ; Murr. Mon. p. 282.
    obliquus Lec. loc. cit.

BRACHYPEPLUS Erichs.
Wiegm. Archiv. 1842, i, p. 148.
B. glaber Lec. Proc. Am. Philos. Soc. 1878, p. 398.

CONOTELUS Erichs.
Germ. Zeitschr. iv, 1843, p. 249.
C. stenoides Murr. Mon. p. 338.
C. obscurus Erichs. loc. cit. p. 252; Murr. Mon. p. 335.
    ? *spissicornis* Fab. (*Stenus*), Syst. El. ii, p. 603.
C. mexicanus Murr. Mon. p. 377.

NITIDULINI.
EPURAEA Erichs.
Germ. Zeitschr. iv, 1843, p. 267.

?

E. monogama Crotch, Trans. Am. Ent. Soc. 1874, p. 76.
E. Hornii Crotch, loc. cit. p. 76.
E. helvola Erichs. loc. cit. p. 273.
    castanea Mels. (*Omosita*), Proc. Acad. ii, p. 106.
E. rufa Say, (*Nitid.*), Journ. Acad. v, p. 180; Erichs. loc. cit. p. 273.
    badia Mels. (*Omosita*), loc. cit. p. 106.
    rotundicollis Reitter, Verhandl. Nat. Verein., Brünn, 1874, (in separata), 34.
E. integra n. sp.
E. ambigua Mann. Bull. Mosc. 1843, ii, p. 256.
E. Erichsonii Reitter, loc. cit. p. 35.
E. rufida Mels. (*Omosita*), Proc. Acad. ii, p. 106.
E. corticina Erichs. loc. cit. p. 270.
E. immunda Sturm, Ins. xv, p. 59, pl. 294, fig. d ; Erichs. Nat. Ins. iii, p. 145.
    infuscata Mäkl. Bull. Mosc. 1853, iii, p. 206.
    flavomaculata Mäkl. loc. cit. p. 205.
E. adumbrata Mann. Bull. Mosc. 1852, ii, p. 336.
E. avara Rand. (*Nitid.*), Bost. Journ. ii, p. 18.
    nubila Lec. Pacif. R. R. Rep. 1857, App. i, p. 36.
E. fulvescens n. sp.
E. linearis Mäkl. Bull. Mosc. 1853, iii, p. 205.
E. truncatella Mann. Bull. Mosc. 1846, ii, p. 514.
    nigra Mäkl. loc. cit. p. 204.
E. planulata Erichs. Germ. Zeitschr. iv, p. 271; Mann. Bull. Mosc. 1852, ii,
    p. 337; Mäkl. loc. cit. p. 204.

??

E. ovata n. sp.
E. peltoides n. sp.
E. æstiva Linn. Faun. Suecc. p. 152; Erichs. Nat. Ins. iii, p. 143.
    convexiuscula Mann. Bull. Mosc. 1843, ii, p. 255.
E. labilis Erichs. Germ. Zeitschr. iv, p. 272.
E. umbrosa n. sp.
E. obtusicollis Reitter, loc. cit. p. 32.
E. scaphoides n. sp.

???

E. luteola Erichs. Germ. Zeitschr. iv, p. 272.

texana Crotch, Trans. Am. Ent. Soc. 1874, p. 76.

(Doubtful Species).

E. macrophthalma Reitter, loc. cit. p. 38.

NITIDULA Fab.
Syst. Ent. 1775, p. 77.

N. bipustulata Linn. Fauna Suecc. p. 148; Erichs. Nat. Ins. iii, p. 158.

N. rufipes Linn. Syst. Nat. i, 2, p. 573.

obscura Fab. Spec. Ins. i, p. 91; Erichs. Nat. Ins. iii, p. 163.

ossium Kby. Fauna Bor. Am. iv, p. 106.

N. ziczac Say, Journ. Acad. v, p. 179.

uniguttata Mels. Proc. Acad. ii, p. 106.

humeralis Lec. Proc. Acad. 1859, p. 70.

STELIDOTA Erichs.
Germ. Zeitschr. iv, 1843, p. 300.

S. geminata Say, (*Nitid.*), Journ. Acad. v, p. 181.

biscriata Reitter, loc. cit. p. 15.

S. octomaculata Say, (*Nitid.*), loc. cit. p. 181.

S. strigosa Schönh. Syn. Ins. i, 2, p. 140; Erichs. Germ. Zeitschr. iv, p. 302.

PROMETOPIA Erichs.
Germ. Zeitschr. iv, 1843, p. 279.

P. sexmaculata Say, (*Nitid.*), Journ. Acad. v, p. 179.

PHENOLIA Erichs.
Germ. Zeitschr. iv, 1843, p. 299.

P. grossa Fab. Syst. El. i, p. 347.

OMOSITA Erichs.
Germ. Zeitschr. iv, 1843, p. 298.

O. colon Linn. Faun. Suecc. p. 151; Erichs. Nat. Ins. iii, p. 167.

O. discoidea Fab. Syst. Ent. p. 78; Erichs. loc. cit. p. 168.

inversa Lec. Pacif. R. R. Rep. 1857, App. i, p. 36.

SORONIA Erichs.
Germ. Zeitschr. iv, 1843, p. 277.

S. guttulata Lec. New Species, 1863, p. 64.

S. undulata Say, (*Nitid.*), Journ. Acad. v, p. 179.

setulosa ‖ Lec. (*Lobiopa*), New Species, 1863, p. 63.

setosa Harold, (Coleop. Heft. iv.

S. Ulkei Lec. (*Amphotis*), Proc. Acad. 1866, p. 376.

THALYCRA Erichs.
Germ. Zeitschr. iv, 1843, p. 305.

T. concolor Lec. (*Amphicrossus*), Agass. Lake Super. p. 223.

PERTHALYCRA n. g.

P. Murrayi n. sp.

POCADIUS Erichs.
Germ. Zeitschr. iv, 1843, p. 318.

P. helvolus Erichs. loc. cit. p. 320.

infuscatus Reitter, loc. cit. p. 94, (ex typ.).

limbatus Reitter, loc. cit. p. 95, (ex typ.).

breviusculus Reitter, Stettin Zeitschr. p. 318.

P. dorsalis n. sp.

ORTHOPEPLUS n. g.

O. quadricollis n. sp.

MELIGETHES Stephens.
Illus. Brit. Ent. iii, 1830, p. 45.

M. saevus Lec. Col. Kans. 1859, p. 6.
M. rufimanus Lec. Pacif. R. R. Rep: 1857, App. i, p. 37.
   maerens Lec. loc. cit. p. 37.
   californicus Reitter, Rev. Eur. Mel. Brünn, 1871, p. 33.
M. mutatus Harold, Col. Heft. iv.
   ruficornis ‖ Lec. Col. Kans. 1859, p. 6.
M. seminulum Lec. Pacif. R. R. Rep. App. i, p. 37.
   obsoletus Lec. (undescribed).
M. pinguis n. sp.

CYCHRAMINI.

PSILOPYGA Lec.
Proc. Acad. 1853, p. 286.

P. histrina Lec. loc. cit. p. 57.
P. nigripennis Lec. New Species, 1863, p. 64.

AMPHICROSSUS Erichs.
Germ. Zeitschr. iv, 1843, p. 346.

A. ciliatus Ol. Encyc. Meth. viii, p. 210; Erichs. loc. cit. p. 347.
   unilineatus Say, (*Nitid.*), Journ. Acad. v, p. 182.
A. niger n. sp.

CYLLODES Erichs.
Germ. Zeitschr. iv, 1843, p. 342.

C. biplagiatus Lec. Proc. Acad. 1866, p. 377.

PALLODES Erichs.
Germ. Zeitschr. iv, 1843, p. 348.

P. silaceus Erichs. loc. cit. p. 350.

CYCHRAMUS Kugelann.
Schneid. Magaz. v, 1794, p. 543.

C. adustus Erichs. Germ. Zeitschr. iv, 1843, p. 346.
C. Zimmermanni n. sp.

CYBOCEPHALINI.

CYBOCEPHALUS Erichs.
Germ. Zeitschr. v, 1844, p. 441.

C. nigritulus Lec. New Species, 1863, p. 64.
C. californicus n. sp.

SMICRIPINI.

SMICRIPS Lec.
Proc. Am. Philos. Soc. 1878, p. 399.

S. palmicola Lec. loc. cit.

IPINI.

CRYPTARCHA Shuck.
Illust. Brit. Ent. 1839, p. 165.

C. ampla Erichs. Germ. Zeitschr. iv, p. 356.
C. strigata Fab. Mant. i, p. 51; Erichs. Nat. Ins. iii, p. 221.
C. concinna Mels. Catalogue, p. 41.
   picta ‖ Mels. Proc. Acad. ii, p. 107.
   liturata Lec. List, p. 30.

IPS Fab.

Gen. Ins. 1776, p. 23.

I. **obtusus** Say, Bost. Journ. i, p. 168.
I. **fasciatus** Oliv. Ent. ii, 12, p. 7, pl. 2, fig. 13; Say, loc. cit. p. 169.
  quadrisignatus Say, loc. cit. p. 169.
  bipustulatus Mels. Proc. Acad. ii, p. 108.
  sexpustulatus Reitter, Verh. Naturf. Ver. Brünn, xii, p. 161.
I. **sanguinolentus** Oliv. loc. cit. p. 8, pl. 2, fig. 14; Say, loc. cit. p. 169.
  rubromaculatus Reitter, loc. cit. p. 161.
I. **confluentus** Say, Journ. Acad. iii, p. 195.
I. **vittatus** Say, Bost. Journ. i, p. 170.
  Dejeani Kby. Fauna Bor. Am. iv, p. 107, pl. 2, fig. 4.
  sepulchralis Rand. Bost. Journ. ii, p. 19.
I. **cylindricus** Lec. New Species, 1863, p. 64.

PITYOPHAGUS Shuck.

Illust. Brit. Col. p. 25.

P. **cephalotes** Lec. Proc. Acad. 1860, p. 377.
P. **rufipennis** Horn, Trans. Am. Ent. Soc. 1872, p. 146.
P. **verticalis** n. sp.

RHIZOPHAGINI.

RHIZOPHAGUS Hbst.

Die Kæfer, v, p. 18.

Rh. **scalpturatus** Mann. Bull. Mosc. 1852, ii, p. 362.
Rh. **cylindricus** Lec. Proc. Acad. 1866, p. 377.
Rh. **dimidiatus** Mann. Bull. Mosc. 1843, p. 300.
Rh. **brunneus** Horn, Proc. Am. Philos. Soc. 1878, p. 308.
Rh. **bipunctatus** Say, (*Colydium*), Journ. Acad. iii, p. 324; Lec. Proc. Acad. 1866,
  p. 377.
Rh. **approximatus** Lec. loc. cit. p. 378.
Rh. **remotus** Lec. loc. cit. p. 378.
Rh. **minutus** Mann. Bull. Mosc. 1853, iii, p. 206.

Notes on the MYCTERIDÆ and other Heteromera.

BY GEORGE H. HORN, M. D.

A number of specimens of MYCTERUS having been lately added to my cabinet, some collected by Morrison in western Nevada, and several others from C. F. Gissler from New Mexico, there is now sufficient material to give the species some definite characters. The following table will enable them to be separated in a preliminary way.

Thorax broader at base, as wide as the base of the elytra.
  Legs in great part and antennæ yellow.
    Posterior legs piceous...**canescens** n. sp.
    All the legs yellow............. ....**scaber** Hald.
  Legs, antennæ and clypeus piceous...................................**concolor** Lec.
Thorax not broader at base, narrower than the base of elytra.
  Legs, antennæ and mouth yellow..............................**quadricollis** Horn.

The above color characters although trivial are constant and answer